BE NOT AFRAID:

INSIGHTS FOR THE *Journey* TO HOLINESS

BY:
CONNIE PORTER

TATE PUBLISHING, LLC

Published in the United States of America
By TATE PUBLISHING, LLC

Book Design by TATE PUBLISHING, LLC.

Printed in the United States of America by
TATE PUBLISHING, LLC
127 East Trade Center Terrace
Mustang, OK 73064
(888) 361-9473

Publisher's Cataloging in Publication

Porter, Connie

Be Not Afraid / Connie Porter

Originally published in Mustang,OK:TATE PUBLISHING:2004

1. Christianity 2. Spirituality

ISBN 0-9759973-7-8 $13.95

Copyright 2004

First Printing: September 2004

DEDICATION

To my God
who makes all things possible

ACKNOWLEDGMENTS

I'd like to thank:

My husband Charles whose strong faith, prayers, and encouragement played a major role in the completion of this book.

My mother Norma Odom, sister Rita Yancey, dear friend Diane Lapointe, all the members of the Community of Faith prayer group, and numerous others whose constant prayers were a source of great encouragement to me.

Deacon Robert Garza and Wilber Waji for their contribution in making this book complete.

May God bless all abundantly.

TABLE OF CONTENTS

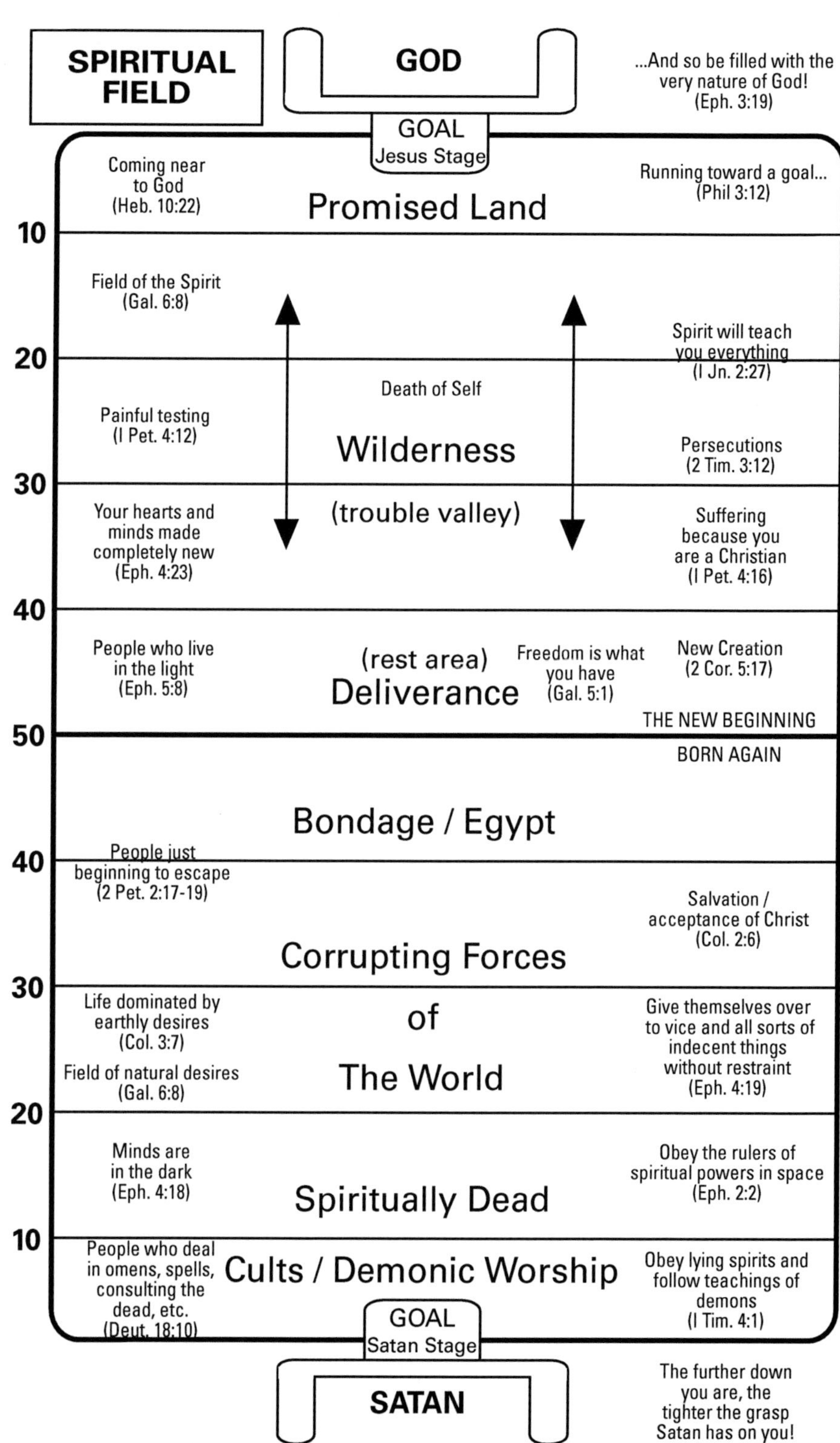

SPIRITUAL FIELD
GOD
GOAL
Jesus Stage
...And so be filled with the very nature of God! (Eph. 3:19)
Coming near to God (Heb. 10:22)
Running toward a goal... (Phil 3:12)
Promised Land
10
Field of the Spirit (Gal. 6:8)
20
Spirit will teach you everything (I Jn. 2:27)
Death of Self
Painful testing (I Pet. 4:12)
Persecutions (2 Tim. 3:12)
Wilderness
30
Your hearts and minds made completely new (Eph. 4:23)
(trouble valley)
Suffering because you are a Christian (I Pet. 4:16)
40
People who live in the light (Eph. 5:8)
(rest area)
Deliverance
Freedom is what you have (Gal. 5:1)
New Creation (2 Cor. 5:17)
THE NEW BEGINNING
50
BORN AGAIN
Bondage / Egypt
People just beginning to escape (2 Pet. 2:17-19)
40
Salvation / acceptance of Christ (Col. 2:6)
Corrupting Forces
30
Life dominated by earthly desires (Col. 3:7)
of
Give themselves over to vice and all sorts of indecent things without restraint (Eph. 4:19)
Field of natural desires (Gal. 6:8)
The World
20
Minds are in the dark (Eph. 4:18)
Obey the rulers of spiritual powers in space (Eph. 2:2)
Spiritually Dead
10
People who deal in omens, spells, consulting the dead, etc. (Deut. 18:10)
Cults / Demonic Worship
Obey lying spirits and follow teachings of demons (I Tim. 4:1)
GOAL
Satan Stage
SATAN
The further down you are, the tighter the grasp Satan has on you!

FOREWORD

Awesome is one of the most appropriate words that I can use to describe the contents of this book. It provides guidance, wisdom, and encouragement for anyone truly seeking the Lord and looking for the narrow road that leads to eternal life.

We are truly living in the darkest times in history. A time where the American dream, the pursuit of happiness, and self-satisfaction have distorted and destroyed the very fabric this country was founded upon. Living in this fallen world can often confuse or cloud the minds of believers in Christ on their quest towards heaven. Standing in the gap between what the world says and what God says can sometimes be an awkward position, leaving even the strongest Christians with questions regarding the meaning of life and where to turn next. Thankfully, the Lord, through his Holy Spirit, continues to inspire individuals to provide helpful information to other Christians that helps make the Journey easier. The Bible says, "Do not store up for yourselves treasures on earth, where moth and rust destroy, and where thieves break in and steal. But store up for yourselves treasures in heaven, where neither moth nor rust destroys, and where thieves do not break in or steal; for where your treasure is, there your heart will be also" (Matthew 6:19–21).

Be Not Afraid will help you find this treasure that the Lord is speaking of. It explains the Journey to Christ in a way that is easy to understand, realistic, and applicable to life today. The author provides scriptural references, pertinent examples, and shares the personal story of her own Journey. It is an excellent source and wealth of information that will encourage individuals to step out of the worlds' way and plant themselves on the path that leads to life. For the Lord says, I am the way, the truth, and the life—*Be Not Afraid* explains the way, will show you the truth, and will ultimately lead you to life.

On my own Journey, I have frequently referred to various parts of this book to help me with different issues. I have always found comfort in knowing where I was on the path and seeing that what I was experiencing at the time was normal and in God's plan. Sometimes the road has seemed so hard that I wanted to give up, but knowing the full realm of what I was working toward has certainly helped me to move forward.

I highly recommend this book to anyone who wants to experience greater growth in Christ. It will answer so many questions about suffering, purification, letting go of the world, and surrendering oneself into the loving arms of God.

Rita Phillips Yancey

INTRODUCTION

It does not take a genius to see that the world in which we live is not such a nice place anymore. The repercussion of sin and selfishness has made life unbearable for many. Apathy, hopelessness, and despair have become serious problems as people search for the meaning of life and solutions to their problems. The sins against God and His ways are widespread, and every one of His commandments is being broken at an alarming rate. The vast majorities of people are no longer concerned with the will of God for their lives and place very little emphasis on prayer, guidance, wisdom, or a relationship with Christ.

Never before in the history of the world has God failed to deal with mankind when it has chosen to ignore His word and pursue its own interests. There are always consequences to sin. It does not matter whether one is speaking of individual consequences or a nation as a whole.

Words such as honesty, trustworthiness, uprightness, truthfulness, integrity and character have become lost in our society as vast numbers of people continue to seek self- fulfillment.

Christians have remained silent for far too long. We have begun to accept this evil all around us as if it were something that we can do nothing about. The enemy has boldly captured area after area of our lives and has successfully corrupted our schools, our media, our entertainment, our political structure, our court systems, our family structure, our relationships, and even some of our churches.

America is a nation that is proud and powerful. It is also a nation without a conscience and a nation that has turned its back on God. The United States, like so many other countries has bought into the lie that, to be happy, you must be successful, wealthy, educated, powerful, and worldly. The American people have now been conditioned to believe that they no longer need God in their lives and that it is not necessary to follow the teachings of the Bible. Large segments of our population balk at God and at the people who choose to follow Him. The language of the average person is foul, his conscience is dead, and his love of God has turned cold.

God in His mercy continues to send warning after warning of the end times only to have them ignored. Hurricanes, earthquakes, drought, floods, and tornadoes are claiming the lives of thousands each year, and statistics tell us that these calamities are on the rise. We, as Christians, can no longer ignore these warnings. We cannot live our lives thinking that since we are not involved in the widespread corruption, that we will not suffer any consequences. This is an error in thinking. The Bible says in Leviticus 18:25 that when corruption is widespread, the land will reject the people who live there. Christians live in this same land and the chastisement that is coming upon our nation will affect us as well.

Jesus tells us in scripture that in the last days, all of the above-mentioned events will be commonplace. Few will say that it is not already occurring, and that it is clearly time for all of God's people to get prepared for the day of the Lord. There is an enormous amount of material available that focuses on the Book of Revelation in the Bible, but far less focus on being prepared for the events described in it.

This book is designed to do just that. I believe that God wishes for his people to be well informed about the end time events. However, I do not believe that it is the Lord's desire for His people to be so focused on these end time events, to the exclusion of everything else scripture mentions, that it leaves them spiritually unprepared for what lies ahead.

One of the things that the Book of Revelation should do for Christians is to open our eyes and allow us to clearly see the dire necessity of walking the straight and narrow path that leads to eternal life. The enemy uses all sorts of tactics to keep the Christian off balance. If he can keep our minds focused on worrying about what is going to happen, he has succeeded in keeping our minds off of being prepared for it.

For over twenty years, I have been on a

walk with the Lord that has taught me many lessons. Perhaps one of the most significant lessons was discovering that God has a specially designed plan for His people. It is a plan that unfolds in stages as an individual walks on his Journey towards the Lord. For those seeking spiritual growth, finding Christian materials written in an easy to understand language that will address common experiences they may have as they advance through these stages can be difficult.

This book is designed to help those who are serious about their spiritual life. It is my prayer, that before you finish this book, you will have an idea of where you are on your Journey, how much ground you have already covered, and how much further you have to go. And as an added benefit, you will also be able to tell where other people are on their Journeys as well.

What you read here comes from scripture. Therefore, throughout the book there will be scripture passages given as an aid for you to clearly see God's plan as it unfolds in the Journey. I encourage you to take the time to read the scriptures as you come across them.

There have been thousands of people who have walked this path before you, and there will be many more who will walk it after you. The one thing people really want to know most of all is exactly what they can expect to happen to them.

There are common experiences that people have as they advance through the different stages. There are also common emotions people experience that can be difficult to understand. For example, it is not unusual for people to panic if they do not feel the presence of God or if they experience aridity in prayer. Both are normal parts of the Journey and everyone who has walked before you has experienced them.

I know, as an ordinary Christian myself, it would have been beneficial to me to know about these common experiences before I entered the stages. The knowledge would have prepared me with insight into what I could expect to happen to me.

As a means to help you understand how the Journey unfolds, there is an illustration shown at the beginning of the book. It lays the Journey out in a diagram like a football field. In studying the stages, you will be able to clearly see God's divine plan for each of His children. When you look at the illustration of the Spiritual Field, you will see a dividing line, which I call the fifty-yard line. Anything above this line is the Holy Spirit's side of the field; anything below it is the field of natural desires, or Satan's side of the field. He controls this area. Anyone who has not invited Christ into his life will automatically fall somewhere below the fifty-yard line.

In regard to the lower stages of the Spiritual Field, much of what you read will not be pleasant because when you are dealing with Satan's side of the field, you are dealing with sin.

However, it can be an eye-opening experience to clearly see who these people are who reside in these areas and what they are doing.

In reading this book, you are about to go on an adventure with Christ. It will at times be challenging and exciting on the one hand, yet painful and sometimes confusing on the other. You will come to understand that no matter how you feel, nothing unusual is happening to you. You will discover that all of God's people who have walked before you have experienced the same things in their spiritual lives.

I had originally intended to start this book by discussing the time when a person begins to have an awareness of Christ. However, in my prayer time, I began to sense that the Lord wanted me to go back to the time prior to when a person experiences salvation. There may be a very good reason for this, since there are some things that people can get involved in before they invite the Lord into their lives that they just cannot walk away from. Figuratively speaking, these things can leave an open door through which problems may enter later on in the Journey.

Matthew chapter 7, verse 14 speaks about the gate to life being narrow and the way that leads to it being hard. It also reveals that few will find the gate. What is this way that the scripture is speaking of, and how can we be sure that we are on the right path at any given stage of the Journey? If we follow this plan, we will find the answers to both of these questions hidden in the words of scripture. So let us begin.

CULTS AND DEMONIC WORSHIP

Who are the people caught up in this stage? Are you able to identify them? It's not that difficult. The Word of God tells us how to do it. God does not want His people to be ignorant, nor does He want us to be immature in our thinking. He wants us to be aware and well-informed. We need to be able to look at the people here and come to terms with who they are and what they are doing. How do we do this? We go to the Word of God, which gives us a good description of the people down here (see illustration).

The Bible says in Ephesians 2:2 that they "obey the ruler of the spiritual powers in space, the spirit who now controls the people who disobey God." Who is this ruler of the spiritual powers? Ephesians 6:12 tells us. "For we are not fighting against human beings but against the wicked spiritual forces in the heavenly world, the rulers, authorities, and cosmic powers of this dark age." These powers and forces are not God. The people living in this stage of the field are not only obeying these forces, but are being controlled by them as well. In Matthew 7:15–20 the Bible warns against false prophets saying, "You will know them by what they do." A prophet is simply a person who gives witness to someone else. John the Baptist was a great prophet. If you recall, in Matthew 3:11 he said, "I baptize you with water . . . but the one who will come after me will baptize you with the Holy Spirit and fire." John was giving a witness to Christ. False prophets give witness to someone too. They give witness to Satan. Their message will lead you away from Christ. The people caught up here are the furthest from Christ and the closest to Satan. You should be able to recognize them. As a Christian, you should be able to recognize where anyone is simply by listening to them and watching what they are doing.

The Bible also says in 1 Timothy 4:1 that these people "will obey lying spirits and follow teaching of demons." Clearly these people are being taught how to further the work of Satan. People involved in witchcraft, Ouija boards, crystal balls, levitation, palm reading, handwriting analysis, ESP, tarot cards, hypnosis, horoscopes, astrology, seances, and psychics have all learned not only how to do their crafts, but how to promote them as well. There is no question that these people are being used by the enemy to give false advice.

Leviticus 19:31 of the Good News Bible states: "Do not go for advice to people who consult the spirits of the dead. If you do, you will be ritually unclean . . ." Everyone in this stage is ritually unclean since these are normal activities for the people here. The same verse in the New American Standard translation says: "Do not turn to mediums or spiritists; do not seek them out to be defiled by them." These are clear warnings against consulting people who present a grave spiritual danger to you and who can render you unclean in the eyes of God. All false religions, yoga, mind sciences, and devil worship are common practices among the people in this category. Be advised that these people, aided by unclean spirits, are capable of doing things that normal people cannot do. God strictly forbids and detests all of the above actions. The people here have lost all feelings of shame and their consciences are dead. Often unclean spirits have cut off their feelings for others as well. This is why they are capable of doing unspeakable acts. Stay away from them; they are deadly to you as a spiritual person.

If you have been caught up in any of these types of activities, you CANNOT just walk away from them. You must confess and renounce them, and then totally repent of them. You then need to make a complete change by turning and going in the opposite direction. It doesn't matter whether you have sought advice from these people (even if it was just a one-time experience), have been in a place where it was happening, or have been with someone who was doing it. Nor does it matter whether you felt that what you saw and heard was insignificant; the bottom line is that you were exposed to the demonic forces and you must therefore take the three steps necessary to be freed from them. Take the time now to confess, repent, and renounce any demonic behavior of these types. By taking these three steps you will shut the door on the evil and you will not have to worry about it coming back and affecting you later on in your Journey. As long as the door is open, Satan can and will use that door to get to you. He does not play fairly. If he can get you, he will. He does not care if you understand the rules or not. Anytime a person seeks advice apart from God and apart from His Word, it is an action that is forbidden by God. As a Christian, you should not be having your palms read, should not be seeking advice from psychics, and should not be reading your horoscope. You are either for God or you are not. You cannot sit and partake in evil at the table of the enemy, and then turn around and sit at the table of the Lord. Fraternizing with the enemy is always a dangerous activity on the part of any Christian.

I believe that people who claim to have true psychic powers, read tarot cards, or contact the spirits of the dead are receiving information, but the source of that information is not God.

Do not be surprised if the Lord is bringing something to your mind now that happened in your past. It is His way of telling you to take the three steps and get it out of your life now.

Unfortunately, activity in all the above-mentioned areas is on the rise in our country at an alarming rate. Many young people, bored with life, are entering the world of cults and demonic worship in droves. Any society that permits music such as heavy metal, sells merchandise such as Ouija boards, games such as Dungeons and Dragons, books on devil worship, witchcraft, satanic activities, horoscopes, tarot cards, etc., is doing a grave disservice to its people because in doing so, it is contributing to the demise of the country. It is also calling down the wrath of God upon a nation.

It is abundantly clear that Satan is controlling the people in this stage. Their products, their message, and their motives are all designed to keep a person under the control of Satan. Their reward will be eternal damnation.

CHAPTER II

<u>Spiritually Dead</u>

If you move up on the diagram a little further, you will find a completely different set of people altogether (see illustration). They are the "Spiritually Dead." Obviously, the people in the "Cults/Demonic Worship" stage are spiritually dead too, but those in this next stage are a little bit different. They may not even be involved in any of the previously mentioned activities. However, included in this category, you will find agnostics, atheists, and people who promote humanism. These are the people who simply will not accept the Word of God. As a result, they have come up with their own theories as to why and how things happen. For example, those who could not accept the creation of Adam and Eve came up with the Theory of Evolution. Since apes are still around, it is highly unlikely that man evolved from them. Once evolution occurs, the former no longer exists. The fact that apes are not extinct proves that the Theory of Evolution is incorrect.

Another good example is those who will not accept that God created the earth. These people came up with the Big Bang Theory. Don't underestimate these people's intelligence and don't shortchange them—they may have more faith than most of us. The reason I say this is because it takes more faith to believe that the earth just fell out of the sky, than it does to believe that someone is responsible for it. It takes more faith to believe that the sun, moon, stars and seasons all function by themselves, than it does to believe that someone is behind it all. These people have some type of faith, but they have it in the wrong place. Their belief system is totally wrong!

Anyone who falls in this category is spiritually dead. You will know them by what they do. When a person is spending an untold amount of time writing books about humanism, faith in man but not in God, and they are dedicated to this, they are spiritually dead. What does this say about the textbooks our children are studying in school? People who are spiritually dead are writing many of these books. Look at the diagram and see just how far away from God they really are! Those of no spiritual faith are using their false beliefs to influence our children while they are still in their formative years. Our government and educational systems are now forcing teachers to talk about sex and alternative lifestyles while forbidding them to talk about God! Every Christian ought to stand up and object to the ban on prayer in American schools and theories that directly contradict the Word of God. It is a national disgrace for the American people to allow the door of God's teachings to be slammed shut while the door to the enemy has been thrown wide open.

It is abundantly clear that Satan is controlling the people in this stage too. He must keep their minds in the dark in order to continue to use them to promote his thinking. Unlike the people in the "Cults and Demonic Worship" stage whose message and activities are repugnant to some, the people in this second stage want to influence your mind in a more acceptable manner. They are really not interested in shocking and bazaar behavior. These people spread deadly messages that are harmful to you as a Christian, yet are presented in a nonchalant, almost logical manner. You must realize that it is in your best interest to stay as far away from people like this as is humanly possible.

CHAPTER III

Corrupting Forces of the World

Everyone on planet earth has been in the "Corrupting Forces of the World" stage at one time or another. You cannot get called out of the world if you have never been in it. So the question now becomes: Where in it were you? There are two different levels to the "Corrupting Forces of the World" stage: the level that exists between the twenty and thirty yard lines and the level that exists between the thirty and forty yard lines. Obviously, the people on the forty-yard line are not as consumed by evil as the people on the twenty-yard line (see illustration).

People on the Twenty-Yard Line

Let us now take a hard look at the people in this stage. What is going on in the lives of these people? How can you identify a person who is here? How can you find out if you have ever been here?

Scripture is quite clear regarding the activities going on among people in this stage. The Word of God says that it is the " . . . field of natural desires . . ." (Galatians 6:8). These people lead lives that are dominated by earthly desires. Their minds are in the dark. They strive to satisfy their human wants. They have goals, but those goals do not include Christ. There is something or someone in the center of their world but it is not Christ.

Sin also dominates the lives of the people here. They enjoy it, embellish and embrace it. Because so many people live at this level, sin has become rampant in the United States and many other countries as well. We see the consequences of rampant sin in Proverbs 29:16, "When evil people are in power, crime increases. . . ." No one can deny that crime has taken a strong foothold in the United States. The solution to the crime problems facing our nation is not to build more jails or to crack down with harsher sentences, but for people to turn away from sin!

The people in this stage will "have no part in the life that God gives, for they are completely ignorant and stubborn" (Ephesians 4:18). Again, we discover who these people are by what they do.

The Word of God says in Ephesians 4:19 that these people "give themselves over to vice and do all sorts of indecent things . . ."

In today's society, there is not only a rise in vices such as drugs, alcohol, and illicit sex, there is also a sharp increase of interest in many perverted activities. According to Ephesians 4:19, these people will not resist temptation and will continue to sin without restraint. They will exercise no self-control at all.

The Bible is the most complete book known to mankind. It will tell you everything you need to know about faith, love, life and the hereafter. The Bible also gives you a good description of the type of perverted activities that are commonplace among the people in this stage. You will find these activities listed in the Book of Leviticus, chapter 18. There are six. We will examine each one later in this chapter.

Throughout the history of the world, there has never been a time when these six things became prevalent in the land that God did not deal with it. He dealt with it in the time of Noah, and with the people in Sodom and Gomorrah. He dealt with it in the Roman Empire, and He is going to deal with it in our time, because most of these perverted activities are prevalent in our land today. In fact, the whole world is becoming a cesspool of these types of sins. The Lord never has and never will accept or condone these types of behaviors. According to the Word of God in Leviticus 18:25, when these acts become prevalent in a land (the key word here is prevalent) God will cause the land to reject the inhabitants who live there.

In order to see the truth clearly, we need to take the blinders off of our eyes, look at these perverted activities, and call them exactly what they are. The practice of calling sin by another name does not change it. For example, to call homosexuality an "alternative lifestyle" is simply a way of covering up sin in an effort to make it acceptable. This does not change it. It is still sin. If it's wrong, it's wrong.

The book of Leviticus lists the following sins as being an abomination to the Lord and as being reason for God to send His wrath down upon a nation.

INCEST

The first perverted sin forbidden by God in Leviticus 18 is incest. Verse 6 says, " . . . Do not have sexual intercourse with any of your relatives." For years, this sin has been taking place in homes across the nation at an alarming rate. It is an abomination to the Lord. Children have a right to be able to grow up without being forced to participate in this unspeakable sin. Unfortunately, not only are they being forced to do horrifically inappropriate things, many will carry the secret of what happened inside them for years. Normally, the victims are damaged for life if they do not obtain the healing power of God. Only in recent years have victims begun to speak out about this abuse. Modern researchers have been able to connect bazaar behavior patterns such as multiple personalities, violent personalities, and many other problems to this particular sin. The perpetrators seek only to satisfy their own desires without regard to the pain that is inflicted on their victims. Incest is one of the most selfish acts known to mankind.

FORBIDDEN SEXUAL PRACTICES

Did you know that scripture forbids a man to have intercourse with a woman during her monthly period? This is the second abomination described in Leviticus 18:19. A woman is considered ritually unclean during this time. People are to abstain from sexual intercourse and exercise self-control during a woman's menstruation.

ADULTERY

The third forbidden sin covered in Leviticus 18 is adultery. Verse 20 says, "Do not have intercourse with another man's wife . . ." Adultery is the root of many social problems in our society today. The fabric of the family is being destroyed daily as married people seek to satisfy their own desires through this abomination to the Lord. It is one of the most common reasons for divorce. Infidelity leads first to the breakdown of the family, then to single parents, rebellious children, crime, poverty, anger, depression, rage, pain, and suffering. This sin is so widespread in our country, that it is truly a national disgrace. Adultery causes pain unlike any other pain on earth, for it is an act of betrayal and a violation of trust. These, I believe, are two of the deepest wounds of the human heart.

Satan has effectively used this sin to

destroy the family. God intended for there to be a mother and a father in the home. There is nothing in scripture that says it is alright with God for a person to abandon his/her responsibilities and to seek self-gratification. The institution of a sanctioned marriage is sacred. In the eyes of God, once married, the two become one. Anyone who deliberately interferes in that union will not escape the wrath of God. Likewise, any mate who violates the marriage bed will suffer equally devastating consequences.

ABORTION

Yet another sin discussed in Leviticus 18 is abortion. Verse 21 says, "Do not hand over any of your children to be used in the worship of the god Molech, because that would bring disgrace on the name of God, the Lord." We don't have a God called Molech, but we do have a God called money. We don't sacrifice our children on altars, but we do abort them. There are millions of infants each year arriving at the throne of God sacrificed at the hands of their parents for a god called money. There is nothing more innocent or helpless than an unborn child. A child is a gift from God—His most precious creation—but children in the womb are being discarded as nothing more than trash.

Abortion is connected to our money-crazed society. Children are often seen as obstacles to attaining the lifestyle many people desire.

The tragedy of abortion is the aftermath; the belief that once the child is aborted life goes on. What society fails to inform the mother is that there is devastation that follows this act. Often times the woman never gets over the experience no matter what she is told. For many of these women, the damage will remain a lifetime unless the healing hand of God touches them.

HOMOSEXUALITY

The fifth sin discussed is homosexuality (Leviticus 18:22). The referenced scripture does not say that it is acceptable in certain circumstances, nor does it support the belief that one's genes or biological make-up causes him to venture into such a sin. Unfortunately, our media has allowed this sin to flood the mainstream of society. Many leaders of our nation have not only condoned the practice, but are actively lobbying for social acceptance of homosexuals as well. This sin, this abomination to the Lord, is being forced upon the American people. Efforts are being made to pressure everyone into accepting these people in the workplace, in the media, in our private lives, and even in the church. Those who reject these efforts are charged with discrimination and are threatened by the law. It is Christian philosophy to hate the sin but love the sinner; however, the Bible does not say we are to accept this sin by any means. In fact, there is not one scripture in the Bible that supports homosexuality. From the very beginning of the Bible, God speaks of creating man and woman, that is, Adam and Eve. It does not say Adam and Adam, or Eve and Eve. Why? God never intended for this to be so. It makes no sense for God to create something that is an abomination to Himself and then condemn a person for being that way. This would be the action of an unfair God, and we do not have an unfair God.

BESTIALITY

Finally, the last abomination covered in Leviticus 18 is bestiality. Verse 23 plainly states, "No man or woman is to have sexual relations with an animal . . ." It isn't difficult to find magazines and books depicting this very act. This is a vile and disgusting practice and those indulging in these acts defy the laws of nature and the will of God.

All of the above sins are sexual in nature and God calls them perverted. People who engage in such acts are unclean in the eyes of God. These actions also make a land unclean and cause the wrath of God to come down upon a nation. The only time in history when such sins were occurring all over the world was in Noah's time. God destroyed everything in a flood in order to cleanse the land and punish the people. The regulations outlined in Leviticus 18 are not suggestions by the Lord. They are commands. His order to the people is DO NOT participate in perverted activities!

These very sins are being committed by the people in the lower stages of the "Corrupting Forces of the World." Clearly large segments of the population are engaging in such behavior. Most of these sins are commonplace in our society and anyone who is involved in them is living a life that is an abomination to the Lord. There are no exceptions!

When these sins become commonplace, God will cause the land to reject the people. Have these sins become commonplace? Yes, unfortunately they have (especially over the last half a century). Take for example, homosexuality. Forty or fifty years ago this sin was almost unheard of in the United States. Those who did practice homosexuality did so in the "closet," not marching down the main streets of America demanding gay rights! Keeping their activities secret was mandatory in those days because such behavior was unacceptable to the average American citizen. Why do homosexuals no longer fear rejections from society as a whole? Could it be that the morals of the average citizen have declined? Have we turned our eyes away from the growing number of people who believe that it is the homosexuals business what they do, not ours? Or has the average citizen become so involved in other perversions that are equally abominable to the Lord that homosexuality no longer stands out above any other sin? What used to be the exception fifty years ago seems to be the norm today.

So has the land begun to reject the people as a result of these sins? Yes, it has! The world's food supply is already threatened by the chastisements from the Lord. Harsh winters, severe droughts, sizzling summers, and early freezes are destroying the very food we eat, and it is happening on a regular basis. I believe that it is safe to say that the land is no longer producing as it once did.

Insurance premiums continue to rise as hurricanes, tornadoes, floods, earthquakes, and fires cause staggering amounts of property damage and kill thousands of people in the process.

What is it going to take for people to realize that the price of sin is God's wrath and that the wages of sin is death? Unless there are immediate changes in the lives of citizens of America and other nations of the world, food prices will continue to soar as more and more crops are destroyed. Insurance companies will begin to refuse to provide coverage for those living in parts of the nation that are continually being devastated. This has already begun in the state of California and other areas of the country equally hard hit by natural disasters. Not surprising when you stop and think about what is coming out of Hollywood these days and the lifestyles of the rich and famous. On the other hand, take a look at places like Iowa and Montana. How often are these states in the news? It doesn't take a lot of intelligence to see that the people in these states are leading drastically different lives that are not calling down the wrath of God upon them.

Another possible outcome of the failure of man to obey God is a nation's loss of power. The United States is already losing its power as a result of sin. While the United States is still recognized throughout the world as a major power, the leaders of our nation are now forced to deal with situations that would have never occurred in the 1950s. A good example of this is that smaller nations used to have a certain amount of respect for the United States because of its power. Many of these nations no longer do. Smaller countries such as Cuba, Iran, and Iraq have all forced the deployment of thousands of American troops, whereas fifty years ago, just a verbal threat from the United States was sufficient to prevent the onset of war.

It is said that history repeats itself, but that man does not always learn from his mistakes. The Roman Empire was the strongest and most advanced nation on earth in its time. However, Rome fell, and I believe it fell because of the sin within it. People engaged in all sorts of vice and indecent behaviors and Rome became a Godless nation where sin was out of control. We need to recognize that it is this kind of thing that the Word of God warns us about. These sins will most assuredly bring a nation to its knees before God.

The Bible also clearly says that the people

involved in these perverted activities will be doing it without restraint. The typical lives of people in this stage will be filled with sin. They will excuse it, embrace it, and enjoy it. Most of the entertainment in the United States comes at the hand of the people in this stage. A steady diet of violence, sex, drugs, adultery, murder, and mayhem has been paraded across the screens of televisions in our nation for years. Good, clean, wholesome entertainment is becoming a rarity in our country and it is a disgrace.

Those in the stages above this level usually find the behavior in this stage repugnant, whereas the people in and below this stage love it. They crave it and find no shame in participating in it

PEOPLE ON THE THIRTY-YARD LINE

As we move up to the next group of people, you will find that, while they are still in the Corrupting Forces of the World" stage, the things that are going on in their lives are different. Just like the previously mentioned groups, these people can also be identified by what they do.

Have you ever met a person who goes to church on Sunday, who keeps the Ten Commandments, is what most would consider a moral person but is someone who has never made a personal commitment to Christ? I know many. The churches are full of them. In fact, I was once such a person. I thought that as long as I was not involved in all the corruption around me that I was a good Christian and would go straight to heaven. I, however, was completely deceived and was enjoying a false sense of security. Because I had not invited Christ into my life nor made Him my personal Savior, I had no real relationship with him, and without a real relationship with Christ there is no way to make it into heaven. Someone who has "good morals" may be a respectable person but is not necessarily a Christian. Christianity goes far beyond this.

The greatest commandment is to love the Lord your God with your whole heart, your whole mind, and your whole soul. Is not the greatest sin, then the breaking of this commandment? Simply going to church is not enough to reach the gates of Heaven. You must love the Lord with your whole heart. Until you have made a personal commitment to Jesus, God is not really in your heart. You are just as lost in this stage (even if you are not all that sinful) as those in the lower stages. This is because you have not truly started your journey with Christ. You are not following Christ. The Bible makes it clear that we are either for God or against God. There is no middle ground. You either do what the Word of God says, or you don't. The people in this stage are not close to God at all. Many go to church out of habit or a sense of obligation, but once they leave the Sunday morning service, they never give another thought to God (or His will) the rest of the week. You cannot say that you love someone and then only visit him or her once on Sunday and ignore him or her the rest of the week. Those who conduct their spiritual lives in this way are merely an acquaintance of the Lord and nothing more.

God, in His love and mercy, will act in a person's life who resides in this level of the "Corrupting Forces of the World." He may use a different method to reach each person, but somewhere in the process the person will be given the opportunity to follow Christ in the true sense of the words. Sometimes a person will begin to have a sense of something, but they will not know what that something is. They might start to have questions about life, questions such as "Who am I really?" or "What is life really all about?" Sometimes they may be experiencing a void. They will typically have absolutely no idea what this void is and they will often run in different directions seeking to fill this void. Finally, (and this is the reason more often then not), it will be a personal crisis that will drive someone to their knees seeking God's intervention in their lives. If you are someone facing any one of the situations just described, do not be surprised if a Christian who has already made a commitment suddenly shows up in your life. Know that when things such as these happen, the Lord is beginning to prepare the ground (your heart) to receive the seed (His salvation). This time period will be followed by "The call to a personal relationship with the

Lord." The choice to answer that call is entirely up to you!

Why is it so important for a Christian to know about these lower stages? Why do we need to be aware of these people and what is going on in their lives? Since we are not involved in any of the activities in these stages, why should we be concerned about them at all? One reason is because it makes our witness for Christ much more effective if we are able to identify with people where they are. Another reason is that it provides us with protection from being unnecessarily exposed to evil.

I do not believe that we should go out and start witnessing to anyone in these lower stages without first discerning where they are. Nor do I believe that we should try to convert anyone against their will. I am fully aware that there are teachings contrary to this way of thinking, but I sincerely believe that we should first take into consideration a few things.

First, I believe that it is very important for Christians to stop and think, "Where on the "Spiritual Field" is this person to whom I am about to witness?" If that person is down in the "Cults/Demonic Worship" stage, the seed is going to fall on some very rocky ground. You may be setting the Holy Spirit up to be blasphemed. This may not be your intention, but if you do start witnessing to people in this category, and you do not have a leading from the Holy Spirit to do so, you will just be operating out of the flesh and thus, will not be effective.

In the next step up from "Cults/Demonic Worship" you will find the agnostics and atheists in the "Spiritually Dead" category. If you start witnessing to these people (assuming that they will let you talk to them at all), what do you think is going to happen? You will be basing everything you say on the Word of God, but since they don't believe it, will you actually be making any difference?

What about the people in the "Corrupting Forces of the World" stage? What will happen if you start witnessing to them? In the lower stages, individuals are engaging in vice and all sorts of indecent things. The reaction you will likely get from people in this stage will again be different from those who are in the "Cults/Demonic Worship" stage. What happens is that usually the people in the "Corrupting Forces of the World" stage will view the Christian as trying to shove Christ down their throats. Instead of responding positively, they will simply start avoiding the Christian. So what has actually occurred is that the Christian has not led anyone to Christ. What he has done though, is defeated his purpose and pushed the person further away. Have you seen this happen? Christians with good intentions, who want to spread the Word of God as Christ has instructed, will fail if they do not understand where the person who they are trying to reach is in their life.

It is imperative to wait for the Holy Spirit to lead you into any activity dealing with witnessing. The ground must be prepared. The Holy Spirit does not want you to take matters into your own hands. He wants you to allow Him to work through you. Allowing Him to do so is what really brings in the harvest.

Witnessing to people in the higher levels of the "Corrupting Forces of the World" stage is usually safe. These are church people who have not made a commitment. Since they have a certain amount of religion in them, they are not likely to blaspheme God because they already know what the consequences are.

In view of this, you can be a far more effective witness if you will just stop and think. You can tell where a person is by what's going on in his life. Many times it is not what you say that wins a person over anyway; it is the way you are. It is what they see in you.

I do wish to stress that I am not saying that God does not send people from the upper stages of the Journey down to the lower stages to minister and witness to people. The fact is He does, but I believe that when the Holy Spirit does this, He has already prepared the ground to receive the seed. Many of these people's lives are out of control. They are so lost that they are looking for a way out. It is the Holy Spirit that opens their eyes and allows them to see their lives for what it really is. It is always good to remember that nowhere in scripture does it say that God sent us to save anyone. God sent His Son, Jesus, to do that. We, as Christians, are simply instruments that God may choose to use to attain the goal of salvation. Scripture does mention that some seeds will fall on rocky ground. If God chooses to send you into a person's life and that person rejects the message, or it doesn't take root, then leave and shake the dust off your feet (Matthew 10:14).

Anyone reading this book, whose mate has not made a commitment to God, should be able to tell where he or she is now. You should also be able to tell where your friends, family members, fellow workers, and acquaintances are as well. Anyone who has not made a commitment to God will fall in one of these lower stages.

In order for you to escape this level of the "Corrupting Forces of the World" stage, the one thing you must do is to make a personal commitment and invite the Lord into your heart. Whereas, others such as your parents, caretakers, etc, may have previously made all the decisions regarding religion (or the lack of it) in your life, the ultimate decision to follow Christ is yours. Once this is done, your spiritual journey has begun. This action will cause the Lord to place your feet on the straight and narrow path that leads to eternal life. The Bible says in Revelation 3:20 "Listen! I stand at the door and knock: if any hear my voice and open the door, I will come into their house and eat with them, and they will eat with me." The door here is your heart. God wants you to say, "Yes I want you to come in." Once this occurs, you will automatically enter the next stage which is "Bondage/Egypt."

It is interesting to note that despite the onslaught of evil that began in the late 1960s when gays came out of the closet, abortion became an issue, and adultery went on the rise, that God did not forsake the world in spite of its sin. The Word of God says in Romans 5:20 that when sin increases, God's grace increases more. Did this happen? Of course it did. God is always true to His Word. Around the time that all of this started happening, there was an outpouring of the Holy Spirit and the rebirth of interest in His gifts. God set forth His hand once again to recover the remnants of His people.

There are literally billions of people on earth today, but there are only a few who are willing to sacrifice whatever this world has to offer and follow Christ. In comparison to the number of people alive, there is only a small number whose hearts are not hardened and whose ears are not dull. There are only a few people who have their eyes fixed on the things above rather than on the things of this world. These are the remnants. These are the true Christians.

Scripture says that Christ will appear twice. The first time was when He came to deal with sin, and to teach us how to conduct our lives properly among other things. The second time He appears, He's coming for the remnant who, according to the Word of God, will be eagerly awaiting Him. It does not take a genius to see that the world is spiraling out of control and delving into all sorts of sin. More and more it will become a place that those who choose to follow Christ will be unable to tolerate. Scripture says Christians will be persecuted, arrested, punished, and put to death. The spread of evil will be so rampant that many people's love will grow cold (Matthew 24:9). It's not a place where Christians will be comfortable, but rather a place where they will be eagerly looking for the coming of their savior.

Christians are the light of the world (Matthew 5:14). For years, we have endured being ridiculed, balked at, laughed about, shunned, and treated with scorn. But once the Lord comes and removes us, there will be nothing left but darkness. It is imperative for those who choose not to be left behind to know how God works in their lives so they can be prepared for that day. God in His infinite wisdom knows what it will take for His people to be prepared. Therefore, He has dictated that each of us will be required to walk the Journey towards Him. It is a Journey that will mold us, teach us, purge us, cleanse us, and prepare us.

Jesus himself says in John 14:3 that He will come back and take His people to himself so that we will be in the place where He is. Our eyes have not seen nor could we ever imagine how beautiful that place is. But that's only part of it. The other part is that we have to be prepared to go.

There is a particular scripture in the Bible that bears mentioning here. It should be foremost in all Christians' minds at all times. That scripture can be found in Matthew 5:48. It states, "You must be perfect—just as your Father in heaven is perfect." We must never stop striving to be like our heavenly Father. Sending each of us on our personal Journey is the process that the Lord uses to mold us and make us into what He wishes us to be.

During this process, we will be purged, cleansed, and purified. There will be times when we will feel good and other times when we will struggle and suffer. There are a host of faults and sins that each of us carries inside every day. God Himself will address these problems before allowing us to move into the place He has prepared for us. For instance, if we have one shred of dislike for someone because of his or her race or culture, that's called prejudice. We might as well get rid of it down here on earth, because we cannot take it with us. If we dislike someone because of his or her religion, we will need to get rid of that as well. God calls people from all denominations and faiths because He does not want anyone to be lost. We must learn to love our neighbors as our-

selves since learning to love people is a requirement for admission to heaven. If we have any bitterness, jealousy, anger, unforgiveness, or pride,
we must get rid of it. Heaven is perfect and we
cannot take any sin with us. On our Journey, the
Holy Spirit will work with us and in us so that we
will become a new creation in Him.

God has a master plan that will do all this
for us. It is called the Journey. Throughout this
entire process, our job is to clear our thinking, to
seek the wisdom of God, and to pore over scripture in order to cooperate with the Holy Spirit.

CHAPTER IV

<u>BONDAGE / EGYPT</u>

Everyone has a bondage. It does not matter what kind of background you came from or what kind of life you live. You either have one now, you have already been delivered from it, or it has not yet surfaced in your life. So the next logical question is: What is a bondage?

A bondage is anything that keeps you down. It is anything that keeps you depressed and upset. It is anything that causes suffering, fear, worry, and anger. It is anything that you are a victim of, but that you can't seem to do anything about. It is also something that only the hand of God can deliver you from.

In Exodus beginning with chapter 3, is the story of the plight of the Israelites. For the Israelites, bondage came in the form of slavery. They experienced a visible bondage that everyone could see, and it carried with it every one of the symptoms mentioned above. The Israelites were the victims and suffered under the most brutal conditions set forth by the Egyptians. They could do nothing about their situation. It took the hand of God to deliver them from their bondage.

Because it happened in the land of Egypt, I shall call this the "Bondage/Egypt" stage.

Slavery exists in very few regions of the world today, so it is not a bondage from which most people will suffer. However, there are modern day bondages that people find themselves in which carry with them the exact same symptoms as those brought on by slavery.

Bondage is an all-consuming problem. It can take away your desire to live by causing you to think about your problem all of the time. Living in bondage can make you feel as though your whole world is collapsing around you. It can cause you to experience intense suffering at the very core of your being and can cause tears to flow on a regular basis. Living in bondage can make you feel like you are in a dark hole and like there is no light at the end of the tunnel. To live in bondage can be devastating and can affect your whole entire life. It can rock your world, shatter your dreams, and rob you of your hopes for the future. It can also cause you to be completely miserable and to have intense feelings of insecurity.

Despite all of these horrible symptoms, if you are living in bondage, God can deliver you. It doesn't matter how bad it is, nothing is impossible for God. He can fix any problem you manage to get yourself into.

From what I have seen, most people's bondages fall into one of three categories. The first is marital. Marital problems can produce worry, fear and suffering. In marriages, you have two adult people involved in one of the most intimate, complicated relationships known to mankind. Both have free will. However, one of the partners may feel trapped and may suffer terribly from what his/her mate is doing. He/she may feel that there is nothing that he/she can do about his/her spouse's behavior.

A second type of bondage that is very common today is financial. Have you ever seen a person who has a good paying job, but for some reason can never get ahead? He or she is always paying bills, always struggling and there really doesn't seem to be any logical reason why this is happening. It is bondage.

Financial bondages will produce the same symptoms of fear, worry, and suffering, and will affect a person's whole entire life. The fear of being in a position of losing everything can and does often cause depression and an inability to focus. People who are bound by financial worry will often be unable to sleep or find any peace. Their jobs can be affected and their hope for the future can be destroyed. We are no longer living in a time where compassion and understanding are commonplace. Rather we are living in a world where greed and money rule.

For people in the United States who are accustomed to obtaining lots of material possessions, and who try to keep up with those whom they know, financial bondage can be caused by their own actions. One reason for this is that we, as a society, have a habit of living above our means. We frequently fail miserably when it comes to self-discipline. If we want something, we will usually go buy it or charge it. In doing this, our finances can become such a problem that it will take the hand of God to fix them.

Sometimes, however, financial bondage is not caused by a person's own actions. In today's society, consolidation of businesses, closures of long-standing companies, downsizing, jobs going overseas, and buyouts are the norm. No longer are people enjoying job security until retirement. In the course of most people's working years, there may be several job changes and even lengthy periods of unemployment. Through no fault of their own, they may find themselves in a financial bondage.

A third type of bondage is emotional bondage. This bondage is becoming more and more prevalent everyday. This is simply because of how our society is and the things that are going on in it. There are a lot of victims of this particular bondage. Incest victims, rape victims, abused children and adults, children of divorce, mates of unfaithful partners, ostracized children, children of negligent parents, and children or mates of alcoholics or substance abusers are all victims of this type of bondage. It isn't hard to see that any one of these victims would suffer from emotional problems. This is a bondage, statistics tells us, continues to rise in our country, as people flock to doctors seeking medication to cope with depression and despair.

There are many people today who are victims of something from their past that they had no control over, and which seems to have put them under a curse that they can't seem to break free from. The results of an experience like this affects the decisions they make, the lives they lead, their feelings about themselves, and their interactions with others. People who find themselves in emotional bondage can spend their whole lives filled with anger, resentment, bitterness, fear, and an inability to trust anyone. Low self-esteem, a sense of worthlessness, and insecurity are also common among these victims, and it will take the hand of God Himself to free them from the consequences of someone else's actions.

As I see it, these three bondages are the most common. However, if your bondage does not fit into one of those categories, here are a few more.

Have you ever met people who seem to have it all together? They have no financial, emotional, or marital problems. Nothing seems to be wrong with their lives. They might even be a very successful person such as a head of a corporation, an executive, or president of a successful business. These people have spent most of their lives working, getting an education, and moving up the corporate ladder. They have ignored God and all he has to offer in order to get where they are. However, once they have acquired the position they sought, it is not uncommon to hear them say, "It sure is lonely at the top." Loneliness is another type of bondage and it is a fairly common one. There is a difference in being alone and being lonely. Many elderly people suffer from the bondage of loneliness due to the fact that their children seek success at any cost, and often fail to spend quality time with their parents. The fast-paced life we live in often clouds our way of thinking about what is really important and what God requires of us. Women also suffer from this bondage. Over and over again you hear them say that there is a shortage of good, moral men. They really don't want to be lonely, but the shortage of eligible men can place them in this bondage.

Yet another type of bondage is lust. This is a big one nowadays. People can be caught up in a bondage of lust and know that it is destroying their lives, the lives of their families, and hurting the people they love; yet still keep falling into the same trap. It can get to the point where they feel like there is nothing that they can do about it. If so, they have a serious weakness in this area. Lust is a bondage that needs to be fed on a continual basis. This is why these people keep falling back into the same trap. Human willpower alone doesn't seem to be enough to overcome it. Sex addicts, adulterers, and patrons of strip clubs are all caught in this bondage. To be delivered from the desire to indulge in this type of activity will undoubtedly require the hand of God to move in the life of the addicted.

Multiple marriages and blended families can cause another type of bondage that is fairly common in today's society—abuse. Seldom is the situation created by a blended family like that of the Brady Bunch. There can be personality clashes and conflicts among family members. There can also be rebellion, resentment, anger, and bitterness that will destroy the foundation of family life. The whole situation created by a blended family, can lay the foundation for a turbulent and stressful home life. God has a reason for everything that He says in the Bible. Scripture says that God hates divorce (Malachi 2:16). If mankind would follow the ways of the Lord, then the bondage that is the result of abuse would not exist. Unfortunately, for some innocent children, abuse is a bondage created for them by their parents. The streets of most major cities in the country are filled with children fleeing from abusive situations created in many of these homes.

All addictions are a form of bondage. Something that started out as just being fun can turn into something that will cause you and those around you great suffering. Drugs, alcohol, and sex are the most common addictions. Oftentimes, people want to stop their behavior, but they are just unable to. They may succeed for a short period of time, but before long, they find themselves right back in the same situation. They know it's destroying their health and causing other problems, but they just can't seem to conquer the addiction on their own. Again, human willpower alone is not enough. For many, it will take the hand of God to free them.

If your bondage still does not fit into one of the above mentioned categories, it may be one that hasn't surfaced in your life yet. The ones mentioned here are all clearly visible. It doesn't take a scholar to see them.

Sometimes, people do not recognize that problems in their lives are really bondages. Therefore, they run in all different directions seeking human solutions that do not work.

One cannot solve a spiritual problem with a human solution; to attempt to do so will only cause frustration and failure.

Many people come to the Lord as a result of their desire to break free from their bondage. If you feel this way, then you are definitely in the "Bondage/Egypt" stage. Usually what happens is that you finally come to a point where you feel like something has got to change if you are going to survive. The situation you are living in becomes unbearable and far too painful to remain in. For instance, if your bondage is marital, your relationship with your spouse can seem to be an impossible situation. Getting up in the morning can be a struggle, and getting through the day an even bigger struggle. You may feel like you have tried everything you know to do, yet the situation remains unchanged. You may come to the painful conclusion that everything you have tried did not work and that you no longer have any solutions that will change anything. A common thought for you as you go through this will be that something has got to happen because the situation simply cannot go on like it is. You will realize that your problem is completely out of control.

These are the type of things that go on in an individual's life during this stage. Without a doubt this is a very painful stage. Although this stage can go on for years, it is a consolation to know that it will eventually pass.

For those of you who come to the Lord out of a desire to escape your bondage, it isn't unusual for you to wonder what else is going to occur in this stage. There are a number of things that happen, but one of the most important is that God will become real to you in a personal way. The length of time between your recognizing the presence of bondage in your life and allowing God to become real to you can vary, but you can definitely count on the Lord making His presence known to you. God uses different methods to reveal Himself, but if you seek deliverance then you can rest assured that He is going to become real in your life. He will no longer be a distant God. He will become very real to you. You will have some type of experience that will leave you with no doubt about the existence of God in your personal life.

I can remember very well when this happened to me. I had a bondage in my life that was causing me great suffering. It had come to a point where I was either going to have to get over that bondage or else that bondage was going to destroy me. I was very unhappy. I believe God called me many years before I actually accepted His calling. The reason I didn't answer His call was because I did not like the Christian image. I'm sure many people will be able to identify with this. I thought that in order to become a Christian, you had to give up all the fun in your life. I believed that Christians spent hours and hours in church praying. I didn't like the idea of walking around with a Bible all the time, standing on the street corners preaching, or distributing tracts to people who really didn't want them. I couldn't see myself doing any of these things. I especially didn't like the notion of only having Christian friends. Because I didn't answer the call, I believe my life went slowly downhill and God allowed it to happen. It took the Lord allowing some very painful situations to occur in my life before I was able to deal with my pride, arrogance, and stubbornness. At the end of a five-year period, I found myself at the bottom of what I call the "pit of pain." If I looked forward I saw problems. If I looked sideways I saw problems. And if I looked backward, it was horrifying. All my dreams were shattered, my heart was broken, and I had no desire to live. Anyone who hits the bottom of the pit knows that they have two choices. It is either up or out because you cannot stay there.

It makes no difference how you get to this place in your life. The fact is that when you are there, it hurts. It has to hurt really bad if you can honestly say that you do not care if you live or die. This is a common feeling for people in this stage because there are so many problems and there doesn't seem to be a solution to any of them.

For me, all of my suffering came to a head one night. The experience occurred about three o'clock in the morning. Everyone in the house was asleep but I was awake. This was not at all unusual since insomnia was a nightly occurrence for me at the time. I remember crying so hard because the pain was so deep. When you cry like this, it is caused by a pain that comes from the very depths of your heart.

I had never had any question in my mind that there was a God—I just didn't know how personal He would get. I remember so clearly saying to the Lord that night, "If you care about me at all, either fix this mess or take me out of it, and I don't care which." I meant every word I spoke that night. There was no way I wanted to go on living like that. At that moment, something came over me. I didn't know what it was, nor did I know where it came from. All I knew was that I began to have a peace within myself. And I thought to myself, *This feels too good to last!* I went to bed and slept for the first time in months. When I got up the next morning I still felt good. *Lord, what's happening to me?* I thought. I hadn't felt this good in years. The problems were still there and nothing had changed, but I felt good!

Shortly after that, the Lord made His presence known to me in a way that would change my life forever. What happened to me was unusual, but the point is that God became real in my life in a personal way. He was no longer a "pie in the sky God" who didn't care about me or my needs. He wasn't a God that someone else was telling me about, or a God I was reading about in a book. He became very real to me following my personal experience with Him.

It all happened one night after prayer group. Earlier in my life, I had been confirmed through the Catholic Church but I had never made the connection between that and the Holy Spirit. At the time of my experience, I was attending a prayer group every week. This was not a noble act on my part, I just had the sense that God wanted me to go and I didn't want Him to punish me for disobedience. I had enough problems, but I still had not pulled completely out of the world. I had a bingo habit which I fed two or three times a week. Prayer group started at six-thirty. Bingo started at seven-thirty. Prayer meeting was over at eight-thirty and half time at the bingo hall started at eight-thirty. So every Sunday night, I would go to the prayer meeting and stay until eight-twenty. At that time I would charge out of the building, hop in my car, drive to the bingo hall, buy my cards, sit down and be ready for the second half by eight-thirty. I never did stay for fellowship with the prayer group. It made me uncomfortable to be around people who did so much hugging. I continued to do this until September 2nd, 1980.

On that particular night, during the prayer meeting, the person who was leading it said that there was going to be two baptisms in the Spirit following the end of the meeting. He invited anyone who wanted to, to stay and pray for those who wished to be baptized. Since by nature I am a very curious person, I decided to stay after the prayer meeting that night and skip my weekly trip to the bingo hall. I thought to myself, *Wow this could be really interesting. I've never seen a person receive the baptism in the Spirit before. There is no way I'm leaving now.*

After the meeting and fellowship was over, some people began to leave. Others retreated to a small room at the back of the church called the Blessed Sacrament. I followed them down the hall. I really wanted a good spot close to the action. I was determined that whatever was going to happen, I was not going to miss it! Once in the room, the first person knelt down and everyone gathered around her in a circle to do the "laying on of the hands." This didn't scare me even though I had never seen it done before. Those gathered around had their eyes closed but I had mine fixed on this lady! To this day, I do not know what I expected to happen, but whatever was going to happen, I certainly had no intentions of missing it. As I stood there, I suddenly began to feel very stupid, and I thought to myself, *If anyone opens their eyes they are going to catch me gawking, so I had better attempt to pray.* So I closed one eye, cracked the other, and began to pray the only way I knew how. I began saying the "Lord's Prayer." No sooner had I uttered, "Our Father," did I hear someone call my name. I turned around and looked behind me but there was no one there. I looked at the people but no one was reacting as though they had heard anything. They were all still praying. I paused for a moment thinking this was very strange, but proceeded to close my eyes and pray again. As soon as I did this the second time, I heard the voice again. It was not a voice that I recognized, but it was powerful. Again I opened my eyes and looked around but it was obvious that no one seemed to have heard anything. By this time the lady had received her baptism in the Spirit and a gift of the Spirit, and I had missed the whole thing. When they were finished, I leaned over to the person standing next to me and asked if she had heard anything. "Oh, she said, you've never heard anyone speak in tongues?" I answered "No, but that is not what I am talking about. A voice, did you hear a voice?" She looked at me as if I had completely lost my mind and said a resounding no! For me, there was no doubt that I had heard a voice calling.

By now, the next person had knelt down to receive his baptism, and the people began to do the "laying on of the hands" again. This time, I was more determined to see the baptism happen. Before I closed my eyes, I made sure that there was nothing behind me or above me. Then I closed my eyes and started praying again. This time the voice came back and said: "I want you to be baptized tonight!" I was startled and thought, "I can't do that!" I had no idea what I had to do to be baptized in the Spirit. I didn't know if I was ready and I hadn't asked these people if they would be willing to pray with me. As my mind raced, the voice broke in again and repeated the same thing. "I want you to be baptized tonight!" By this time I was beginning to have a sense of who this really was. I knew that what was happening here was something out of the ordinary. So in my mind, I asked the Lord: "Is this you?" I didn't get an answer. Finally I thought to myself, *Look I have got to get some kind of control here*, (because in this stage you do want control in your life.) I didn't yet know anything about surrendering to God. So I asked the Lord, "If this is really you, you see that man over in the corner? Tell him to come and ask me if I want to be baptized." By this time, the second person had received his baptism in the Spirit and the gift of tongues, and again I had missed the whole thing.

Now everything was going back to normal, at least the normal I knew. I was no longer hearing a voice and had no sense that something was there. Everyone was relaxed. Everything was fine until the man in the corner began to move! And he was moving towards me! I began to back up but he continued to walk towards me. So I thought: "Maybe he just wants a hug, I know he could not possibly know what I was thinking."

He continued to walk straight up to me and said: "Is there anyone else who would like to be baptized tonight?" Without saying a word, I immediately dropped to my knees and received my baptism and the gift of tongues that night. This was followed by a spiritual high that lasted about two months. Do you really believe that after an experience like that, that God wasn't real to me? He was a personal God now!

Of course it doesn't happen this way for everyone. Over the years, I have heard people give testimony about how God became real in their lives. Some said that He physically touched them; others said that He spoke to them through scripture, or answered a particular prayer that let them know, without a doubt, that He took a personal interest in their lives.

No matter what method God chooses to use, there is no question that your heart will be touched in a very special way, and it will leave you with absolutely no doubt that God is real.

Following this experience, you can expect

three things to happen. You will have a new thirst for God, scripture will become alive to you, and lastly, your personal relationship with God will truly begin.

Because of your bondage, your prayers will be mostly petitions in this stage. God fix this, God do that, God please, please, please fix this mess! This is normal. Not only will your prayers be mostly petitions, but at this stage your prayers will also be mostly selfish as well. God understands this though and He wants to free you from all of the ugly things that are going on in your life.

After the baptism in the Sprit, it is common for people to experience a spiritual high. Those who have passed through this stage know that this experience is temporary. They also know that the spiritual high is such a good feeling that they are not ready to let go of it when it begins to fade away. For many people, what they do at this time is what I call "prayer group hopping." They run from one prayer meeting to another or from one Bible study to another, or any other gathering of Christians in an effort to hang on to that feeling. You should know that it is never God's intentions for you to remain in the same place spiritually no matter how good it feels. The idea here is for you to continue to move forward.

Another characteristic of this stage is that you will be blindly obedient to Christ. If you even sense that God is telling you to do something, you will do it. Take a look at this point in the Journey (see illustration). You are not even on God's side of the field yet. You have absolutely no idea about discernment or anything else. Most of what you are hearing is not coming from God anyway, but if you think it is, you will usually act. This blind obedience will be traded for something even better later on in the Journey.

Another symptom is that you will be rigid. What does that mean? It means that you have just begun your new life in Christ and you do not yet know much about God or His ways. You still have a lot of learning to do and much to experience ahead of you. In reference to your bondage, being rigid means that you have not learned to trust God to provide you with a way out where there seems to be no way.

You will often see God's hand in this stage as He begins to fix the problems in your life. The result is that your faith will begin to grow. Being rigid is common. You have just walked into a new life. You have come out of the world and most of what is happening in your spiritual life is not familiar to you. It is not unusual for you to fear what you do not understand.

If we take a look at scripture, we can see very clearly how the Israelites also had this rigidity. When God used Moses to lead the people out of Egypt, he led them to the Red Sea. When their backs were up against the sea and the Egyptians were coming, they saw no way out of that situation (Exodus 14:10). They hadn't learned to trust

God to provide a way out where there seemed to be no way. As is God's nature, He delivered the people in a way that you would never think possible. The Israelites never dreamed that God would open up the sea and let them walk through on dry ground (Exodus 14:16). But He did, and He will deliver His people who live in bondage today just as miraculously. The Lord will even do battle for you! (Exodus 14:14). A prerequisite for getting out of the "Bondage/Egypt" stage is learning to trust God, and you will not get out until you do.

A very real symptom of this stage is you may find yourself in a position where you simply cannot pray. You may find yourself hurting terribly and may feel like things look pretty hopeless. It is quite common to have this experience. I believe that I would have never gotten out of this stage if God had not put other Christians in my life at that time. Christians who were further along in the Journey pulled me through. Their faith and prayers were necessary for me to proceed in my personal Journey. Community becomes very important at this point. Sometimes you don't even have enough faith to pull yourself through and so it is crucial that you surround yourself with those who do.

God will act on the faith of another in your circumstances. God will heal on the faith of someone further along in their walk with Him. We know this from scripture. In the Gospels, we read that a Roman soldier had a servant whom he cared about. The servant was sick and suffering. The Roman soldier went to Jesus and asked him to heal the servant. Jesus said that He would, however, the soldier didn't feel worthy of having Jesus come to his home. The soldier had great faith and believed that Jesus could heal his servant even though the servant was not even there and so he asked Jesus to simply "say the word" and trusted that the healing took place. The soldier's request was answered and the servant did receive a healing on the faith and actions of the Roman (Matthew 8:13). If you are in the "Bondage / Egypt" stage, you too can get help through difficult situations on the faith of someone who is in a higher stage of the Journey.

Clearly if you have any of the above described symptoms in your life, you are in the "Bondage/Egypt" stage. The whole idea here is to expose you to the experiences of those who have walked before you so that you can grow.

There is one other thing that bears mentioning for those of you in this stage. The Lord will typically send a Christian into your life, and most likely that Christian will be somewhere in the "Wilderness" stage of his walk with the Lord. The Lord will use that person as a vessel to pray with you, listen to you, and help you to see some spiritual truths. It will not be uncommon for you, as the younger Christian, to begin to lean on the mature Christian and to use them like a crutch. You will very likely go to that Christian with things that you really should be going to the Lord with. If this happens, you can count on the Lord to remove the mature Christian from your life as soon as you cross over into the Spirit's side of the field. The reason is because you must learn that your source for everything is Jesus Christ. People are only vessels. From the moment you step on to the Spirit's side of the field you will only be permitted to lean on Jesus.

I don't expect people to believe anything I say unless I can back it up with scripture. I don't want you to take my word for it; I want you to see it with your own eyes. It is a very good idea to get in the habit of testing everything you hear spiritually against the Word of God.

Is the "Bondage/Egypt" experience something that just happened to the Israelites in the Old Testament, or is this something that still happens to people today? Does the experience of the Israelites contain a message for all Christians?

If you have any knowledge of scripture, you know that the Israelites' bondage was slavery. If you do not know this, then it would be a good idea for you to stop here and take the time to read the book of Exodus. It would be helpful for you to understand the plight of the Israelites and to see how God worked in their lives to free them so that you can better understand how God can work in your own life. For those of you who are knowledgeable about the story, you know that the situation became unbearable for the Israelites under

Egyptian rule. You know that God became real to the Israelites through the plagues and the pillar of clouds and fire among other things. You also know that the Israelites were rigid and had to learn to trust God to provide a way out where there seemed to be no way. The Book of Exodus tells us that all the signs of this stage did happen to the Israelites. This event happened before Christ, however. Wouldn't it be interesting to know if an event like this ever happened after Christ? Was there ever someone who lived after Christ who experienced the "Bondage/Egypt" stage? Someone who, not only lived in bondage, but who experienced all the symptoms of this stage as well? Let's turn to the Book of Acts chapter 9, and take a look at St. Paul's conversion experience.

St. Paul was one such person. He lived after Christ and his experience in the "Bondage / Egypt" stage was separate from the Israelites experience. His experience involved the baptism in the Holy Spirit. The Israelites did not experience this because the Holy Spirit had not yet come. For both the Israelites and modern day Christians, the conversion experience starts in the "Bondage/Egypt" stage.

It is imperative that you understand that accepting the Lord as your Savior and experiencing the baptism in the Spirit are two entirely different things. Being saved means that you have accepted the Lord as your personal Savior. It is your response to "The Call" that was responsible for your moving up to the "Bondage/Egypt" stage. The baptism in the Spirit is being born-anew.

There is only one baptism in the Spirit, but there are two ways in which a person can experience it (although both ways may be experienced at the same time). You can either receive the indwelling of the Spirit or you can have the further, "Pentecost" experience, which is the outpouring of the spirit, or, as many prefer—the baptism of the Holy Spirit. There is a definite difference between these two ways. What is the difference? If you will read the Gospel of John chapter 20, starting with verse 19, you will see that after the Lord's death and resurrection, He appeared to the apostles. Verse 22 says that He breathed on them and said: "Receive the Holy Spirit." At that moment, they received the Holy Spirit. However, if you look at the beginning of the Book of Acts, Jesus again is speaking to the apostles saying to them: "Do not leave Jerusalem until the power from on high comes upon you" (Acts 1:4). Why did He say this? Did they not already have the Holy Spirit? Yes, but up until that point all they had was the indwelling of the Holy Spirit; they had not yet experienced the manifestations of gifts at that time. This was quite noticeable, for there was no boldness (they were still locking themselves behind closed doors) and there was also no power. The Holy Spirit was in them but had not been released. The release came at Pentecost. When the tongues of fire came down, Peter came out of that room. He was no longer afraid. The apostles didn't speak in tongues when they first received the Spirit. That gift is clearly explained in the Book of Acts as occurring immediately following the Pentecost experience. The people present heard the apostles speaking in their own languages even though there were a variety of languages among them. This is why Jesus told them not to leave Jerusalem until the power came. They needed to wait until the Holy Spirit was released in them before they did anything. The first time, when Jesus breathed on them it was the indwelling of the Spirit that they received. The second time, when the tongues of fire came down upon them it was the outpouring that they received. So if you have experienced the indwelling of the Spirit but do not speak in tongues, don't let anyone tell you that you are not baptized in the Spirit. You may just have the indwelling of the Spirit, or it may just be that speaking in tongues is not a gift that the Lord has chosen to bestow upon you. Not everyone who is baptized in the Spirit speaks in tongues. There are other signs as well.

I find that this explanation is necessary because many people (once they get out of the "Corrupting Forces of the World" stage) immediately begin to try to teach. To be perfectly honest, I am not sure what they are trying to teach. Not only have they just started their own Journey, they are still in bondage. They still have so many problems of their own to sort through that they are not really in a position to minister to anyone. If they only have the indwelling of the Spirit, they will get themselves in situations they will not know how to handle because they are operating over their heads. People like this are likely to cause more problems for themselves and others by getting into situations that they are not prepared to handle. If they do not have the power released in them, they are operating on what they think, not on God's power. Does anyone really need that?

Having said this, we are now ready to go back to scripture and look at the conversion of St. Paul to see if he experienced the symptoms that are common in the "Bondage/Egypt" stage.

St. Paul was Roman by birth. He came from a family of Pharisees. (If you recall, the Pharisees were one of the groups who gave Jesus the most trouble.) Out of all the different sects at the time, the Pharisees were the strictest. They practiced open conformity to the Mosaic Law. They did not believe in this man Jesus, nor did they believe in his followers.

St. Paul was an educated man and is believed to have come from an influential family. St. Paul despised the crucified Messiah, and regarded his followers as being both politically and religiously dangerous. He was filled with anger against them right up until the very moment of his conversion. He honestly believed that it was his religious duty to persecute the Christians. He spoke more than one language and had a good knowledge of scripture too.

The first question one needs to ask regarding St. Paul's experience in the "Bondage/Egypt" stage is "Was he in bondage?" Scripture does not specifically say that he was, but we know that Satan had him bound and was working to use him to try to destroy God's people. He was not experiencing the abundant life the Lord promised. Something was keeping him down. His distaste for Christians was so great, that he was being used mightily by the enemy and he didn't even know it. He was so deceived that he thought he was doing the right thing. At the time of his conversion, St. Paul was actively searching for Christians in order to bring them back to Jerusalem to persecute them.

Turning to scripture now, in Acts chapter 9, verses 3–6, we see that Saul, also known as Paul (see Acts 13:9) is on the road to Damascus. "As Saul was coming near the city of Damascus, suddenly a light from the sky flashed around him. He fell to the ground and heard a voice saying to him, 'Saul, Saul! Why do you persecute me?' 'Who are you, Lord?' he asked. 'I am Jesus, whom you persecute,'" the voice said. We now see another symptom of the stage. Jesus became real to him on a personal basis. Reading on, we see that Jesus continued to speak to him and said: "But get up and go into the city, where you will be told what you must do." The voice did not tell him what was going to happen, the voice only told him to get up and go. St. Paul got up and went to Damascus. Since he was blinded by the experience, his traveling companions, under his direction, lead him to the city. He was blindly obedient to God. Remember, this too is a symptom of the stage.

The Israelites experienced the same thing. God showed them through Moses that He was real. They had no questions about this after all the plagues that came upon the Egyptians. Also, through Moses, God told the Israelites to get up and pack their bags for the time of their deliverance was at hand. The Israelites got up, packed their bags, and left Egypt taking all the wealth of Egypt with them (see Exodus 12:31–36). True to the symptoms of this stage, they too were blindly obedient.

Continuing to read in Acts, chapter 9, verses 10–18, we see, "There was a believer in Damascus named Ananias. He had a vision, in which the Lord said to him, 'Ananias! . . . Get ready and go to Straight Street, and at the house of Judas ask for a man from Tarsus named Saul. He is praying, and in a vision he has seen a man named Ananias come in and place his hands on him so that he might see again.' Ananias answered, 'Lord, many people have told me about this man and about all the terrible things he has done to your people in Jerusalem. And he has come to Damascus with authority from the chief priests to arrest all who worship you.'" Clearly Ananias did not want to go. He knew that St. Paul had a notorious reputation, and certainly did not want to go and confront this man. However, "The Lord said to him, 'Go, because I have chosen him to serve me, to make my name known to the Gentiles and kings and to the people of Israel. And I myself will show him all that he must suffer for my sake.'" At that point, Ananias decided to obey the Lord. St. Paul had already gone through the beginnings of his conversion. He no longer believed as he once did. He had found God and discovered that Jesus is Lord. In verse 18, we see that he experienced another symptom of the stage. He received the baptism in the Spirit!

We have now covered four symptoms of the "Bondage/Egypt" stage. We have bondage, God becoming real, blind obedience, and baptism in the Spirit.

Verse 20 of Acts chapter 9 tells us that St. Paul stayed for a few days with the believers in Damascus. He went directly to the synagogue and began to preach that Jesus was the Son of God. Something clearly happened to him on his way to Damascus. Before, he didn't believe in Jesus or his followers. After his experience, God was real to him, he had a new thirst for God, and scripture became alive to him (all three are symptoms of this stage). The conversion that happened to him is the same thing that is going to happen to you and the same thing that people before you experienced. You can clearly see these symptoms in the account of St. Paul's conversion.

All that St. Paul experienced put him in a precarious situation. He couldn't go back to what he came from because he knew that wasn't right. He had to reject everything that he knew before, including all his friends. If he chose to return to Jerusalem the hunter would have become the hunted.

What happened to St. Paul here? For one thing, although he had made it into the "Bondage/Egypt" stage, all of his friends back in Jerusalem were still in the stages below him. Their thinking, like St. Paul's before his conversion, was not only all wrong, but now that St. Paul was a Christian, they were a threat to his safety and would prove to be dangerous if he returned because they held just as strongly to their beliefs as St. Paul used to hold to his. Of course, he couldn't go forward either, since the Christians did not trust him. If you continue reading this passage in Acts, you will see that some of the Jews tried to kill him at that time (see Acts 9:29). What was he going to do? Remember that one of the symptoms of this stage is that the person is rigid because he hasn't learned to trust God to provide a way out where there seems to be no way? St. Paul was basically in a no win situation. He was like a man without any people. How was he going to get out of this situation? He had just met the Lord and had not learned to trust God yet.

Even though his personal relationship with God had just begun, St. Paul did know how to pray (Acts 9:11). It isn't hard to believe that in this predicament, St. Paul was probably doing a lot of praying. However, he had not yet arrived at the place where he was content doing what God wanted him to do no matter what. He still had a lot of self left in him. Common sense tells us that he would have been very concerned about his safety. It also isn't hard to believe that his prayers were probably mostly petitions.

We can clearly see then that St. Paul had the characteristics of the "Bondage/Egypt" stage. He, like everyone else, could not skip stages. As painful as it is, everyone is still required to go through each stage of the Journey.

Everyone who reaches this point in the Journey should know that the desire to turn back can be very tempting as you begin to experience the symptoms of bondage. The worst thing you can do though is to go back to the "Corrupting Forces of the World" stage. God did not want the Israelites to do it, nor did he want St. Paul to do it. This is a clear message for all believers. As long as you have a free will, you can choose to do whatever you wish. There are people who will decide to go back to the "Corrupting Forces of the World" stage (see 2 Peter 2:20–22). With the Israelites, God chose to lead them by different routes through the desert to prevent them from wanting to return to Egypt (Exodus 13:17–18). However, your free will is something that God will not take away from you. You can choose to return to the "Corrupting Forces of the World" stage if you want to, but be advised if you do choose to go back, you should know that the Bible says you will be worse off than you were before.

"Bondage/Egypt" is a very painful stage, and most people want to know what it will take for them to move on to the next stage. The answer is the same thing that got the Israelites out of bondage, and the same thing the got St. Paul out of bondage—that is, deliverance. Deliverance means freedom from bondage.

Following St. Paul's conversion, whatever bondage that once caused him to be in a position for Satan to use him so mightily, was now gone. He had been delivered! The Israelites' deliverance was not quite so cut and dry. In fact, they weren't truly delivered from bondage just by leaving Egypt. They were delivered only after they crossed over the Red Sea and God closed the water over their enemies—that is when they saw the Egyptians no more. Why did deliverance not occur until this point? Deliverance requires trust. The Israelites were tested over and over again until God felt that they trusted Him and then He opened the Red Sea and allowed them to walk through on dry ground. If they didn't trust God then, they would have remained on the wrong side of the Red Sea and still in bondage. If you don't learn to trust God, you too will remain in bondage. After this event, the Israelites were truly free, but where were they? They were in the wilderness. The next stage up is the "Wilderness."

By now, you should know whether or not you have been through the "Bondage/Egypt" stage. If you have, you would have received most of your guidance from other Christians. Think back, and you will realize that there was another Christian in your life at the time that you were in that stage. A Christian put there by God. If you have been through this stage, you may well be the person God has decided to send into someone else's life to help him. If God does choose to use you as a vessel to help others in the "Bondage / Egypt" stage, whatever you do, don't give them spiritual meat. These people just came out of the world and they cannot handle it. Remember that they have a bondage in their lives. They are hurting! An awful lot of well-meaning Christians who God sends down to this stage to help someone, give that person so much meat that he becomes completely confused. Don't do that. Remember that God wants us to help others with the same kind of help that we received from God (2 Corinthians 1:4). If God didn't want someone giving you too much meat, he doesn't want you to do it to someone else. In following God's specially designed plan, that person will grow anyway, but it will take time.

If you are in the "Bondage/Egypt" stage and recognize the symptoms, whatever you do, don't go back and ask the people in the "Corrupting Forces of the World" stage for advice. Their minds are in the dark. They are being controlled by human desires. Why would you go ask these people for advice? For example, if a person has a marital bondage, and they experience a situation in which they do not know what to do, if they go back and ask the people in the "Corrupting Forces of the World" stage for advice, more than likely, they will be encouraged to get a divorce. This isn't what God wants you to do! God wants you to surrender your problems to Him. The reason so many people stay in this stage for such a long time is because they do go and seek advice from the people in the stages below where they are, and begin to take matter into their own hands. Doing this creates a stumbling block every time. If you need advice, at least go to someone who is headed in the right direction, someone whose mind has already been converted because in doing so you are more likely to receive advice that will help you. Any advice given to you by anyone who is anywhere below the "Bondage / Egypt" stage, will be of no use to you at all.

There is a problem which may occur for many new Christians in the "Bondage/Egypt" stage. Like St. Paul, new Christians may discover that everyone they know—their family, friends, and associates—are all somewhere below them on the Journey. This means that they cannot seek advice from them. If they do, it will accomplish one of two things. It will either pull them back into the "Corrupting Forces of the World" stage, or it will cause them to stray from the will of God.

If you, from the description of this stage, have not even hit it yet, you are in desperate need of prayer because this means that you have not even begun your Journey.

I've been through the "Bondage/Egypt" stage. I have experienced all of these symptoms in my life, and because I did, as painful as it was, I can now stand before any man, any place, and I can say without hesitation, and without doubt, that my God is God.

CHAPTER V

THE SATAN FACTOR

There are two sides to every situation. For the Christian, there are two sides of what is happening to us. There is that which the Lord is doing and there is that which the enemy is doing. It is foolish and childish to try to get past the "Bondage/Egypt" stage by ignoring what the enemy is doing.

When Jesus walked the earth, much of his ministry dealt with evil. Many people would like to think that when Jesus died, rose, and went to Heaven that Satan gradually disappeared. Obviously, this is not true. He is alive and well and roaming planet earth looking for people to devour. And, he is most definitely out to stop us from making our Journey with Christ. He will do everything he can to prevent us from succeeding.

So, wouldn't it be helpful for all of us to know the common pitfalls that we may experience? I know it would have been beneficial to me. I think I fell in every pit Satan dug for me because I did not realize the he was there. He likes to work anonymously. He doesn't even want you to know he is there. He likes to work under the cover of darkness. So we need to expose him and bring to light some of the common tactics he uses.

Going all the way back to the first stage, we will take a look at some of the normal tactics that he uses to discourage, stop, or frustrate our efforts to follow Christ.

The further down on the diagram you are (see illustration), the closer to Satan you are and the tighter the grasp he has on you. Nothing needs to be said about the people in this bottom stage except that they are possessed by the very nature of Satan. He is working through them.

From the ten-yard line all the way up to the forty-yard line, the primary way Satan works is through deception. Deception has many faces. In other words Satan doesn't deceive in just one way.

The most common way that he deceives those on the ten-yard line is to convince them into thinking that life on earth is it! He convinces them that there is no Heaven, no Hell, and that man is the master of his own destiny. The people here, you will recall, are the agnostics, atheists and people who believe in humanism. To deceive someone simply means to cause one to believe something that is false as if it were true.

If we move up the field a little further, we have the people who live in the "Corrupting Forces of the World" stage. In the lower part of this stage are the people who are giving them-selves over to vice and indecent things. For these people the deceit is going to come out something like this: Eat, drink, and be merry for tomorrow you may die. Notice there is no mention of God. Satan wants people to keep their eyes fixed on the things that are happening right now. Have a good time. Live in merriment is the message that the world gives. If it feels good, do it. Never mind if it's going to kill you. AIDS is a good example of this. The world says to go ahead and have intimate relations with as many partners as you can or want to. Never mind if doing so is going to destroy your life, your family, and everything else you have acquired. Adultery is another good example of this one. The world says there's no harm in having a little fun on the side. What your spouse doesn't know won't hurt him/her. Never mind if cheating on your spouse is going to steal your peace, happiness and your hope for the future. If it feels good, do it. That's the world's message and Satan deceives the people in this stage into thinking that they can achieve happiness doing all of these things. The Bible says in 1 Peter 5:8 that the devil is roaming around the earth looking for someone to devour. Roaming is an action word. It does not denote that he is idly standing by. Satan is constantly on the prowl and for most of the people in this stage, he is succeeding at devouring them, and they don't even know it.

Moving up a little further on the diagram, (yet still in the "Corrupting Forces of the World" stage), we run into the people who are not totally bad and who may go to church on a regular basis yet are people who have not made a true commitment to God in their lives. Satan is not going to tell these people that there is no God! It wouldn't make sense. Why would he tell them there is no God? He's got to tell them something different. (You may remember that he told you this too, and you believed if for a time.) What he tells these people goes something like this: "You're all right, you are not bad. You go to church. You're not caught up in indecent things. If you die, you'll go to heaven." This logic creates a false sense of security. Without a commitment to God, the person is not all right.

Now we come to the part of the "Corrupting Forces of the World" stage where the person begins to have an awareness of Christ. From the time that you originally sense God calling you until the time that you are delivered from bondage, you are walking into a major attack area. This is one of the most active times you will experience throughout your entire walk. Why? First of all, Satan doesn't want you to answer the "call." It makes sense for him to start pulling out some heavy artillery to prevent you from doing it. However, if he cannot stop you from going forward, and you actually make it up to the "Bondage/Egypt" stage, he is going to pull out even more heavy artillery because he doesn't want you to be baptized in the Spirit since that gives you power through Christ. Second of all, Satan doesn't want you to be delivered. Why?

Because once delivered, you are on the Spirit's side of the field and it will be harder for him to pull you back. He wants to get to you before you cross over while it is not too difficult. His entire plan is designed to keep you from going forward. He wants you to turn around and go back to the "Corrupting Forces of the World" stage where he is the boss and in control. Moreover, if he does not stop you from answering the "call," he then has to be concerned about all the people who might decide to turn their lives over to the Lord after they see what has happened in your life—and this of course would be a much bigger job.

For those of you in the "Bondage/Egypt" stage, there are four primary ways in which Satan works. He works through your thought processes, your feelings, the circumstances of your life, or the people in your life.

How does Satan work through your thought processes? He causes you worry, fear, and frustration and he keeps you in constant turmoil with his rhetoric. Planting thoughts has been an effective tool of his for centuries and he will continue to do this as long as it works. I will use marital bondage as an example here. Anyone who lives in marital bondage is most likely bound by insecurity. This insecurity can leave a marriage on uneven ground and can cause each partner to be unsure about everything. This insecurity coupled with the fact that the person is no longer associating with anything he knew while in the

"Corrupting Forces of the World" stage, creates a great opportunity for Satan. He will use this situation to plant thoughts in the person's mind that will make him think it's hopeless and that God really can't fix the problems in his marriage.

For those of you who already know that God can fix the problems in your life, Satan comes at you differently. You are deceived into believing that although God may be capable of fixing your problems, He will not do it for you. If the enemy succeeds in getting you to think this, it will make your stay in the "Bondage/Egypt" stage much more difficult. Remember, you must learn to trust God before you will ever get out of this stage. If Satan can convince you that you cannot trust God to free you, then he has succeeded in keeping you in this stage that much longer. Satan is the father of all lies. Everything he tells you is a lie. God is the same yesterday, today, and forever. He has been in the business of delivering His people from all kinds of bondages for centuries. There is no question in my mind that he is close to the brokenhearted and not only *wants* to deliver them from their bondage but *will!*

Frustration is a major way in which Satan works through a person's feelings. The definition of frustration is to prevent, thwart, hinder, baffle, or block. You can count on him to use any one of these methods to get to you, and as long as it works he will continue to use it. It is not until you realize that this is the way Satan is working that you can turn the tables on him. When you begin to reject the temptation to get frustrated, you begin to frustrate Satan and force him to seek another way to keep control over you. Remember he will only use a method as long as it works.

Although you may not realize it, Satan is behind many of the painful situations and circumstances that are taking place in your life in this stage. If you are experiencing any of the symptoms mentioned above, you are in desperate need of prayer. Since there are other Christians in your life, you need to take advantage of their presence and request that they pray for you.

Another common way in which Satan attacks those of you in the "Bondage/Egypt" stage is through the people in your life. He'll often use a friend, a relative, a co-worker, or a neighbor whose life seems to be going really good to make you think that no one else has the problems that you do, and that no one is as unhappy as you are. He wants you to feel really bad about your situation and to make it seem like no one else is suffering like you are. In other words he wants you to wallow in self-pity. This is not from God. (If jealousy becomes an issue, Satan is usually behind it too.) It is good to remember that things are seldom as they seem. The other person's life is probably not as great as what you think it is. Satan wants you to see only the good things that are happening to them, and only the bad things that are happening to you. If you buy into this, he will have succeeded in keeping you upset all the time.

Yet another tactic of Satan is to make you feel that you are being treated unfairly. Does this sound familiar? Every Christian who has walked before you has experienced situations in his life that were very difficult. Nothing unusual is happening to you. Yet Satan wants you to believe that no one has had the problems that you have and that no one has been treated as unfairly as you are being treated. This, too, is designed to keep you upset. Anytime you are despondent, apathetic, full of despair, and feel that the situation is hopeless, you can be sure that you are being attacked by Satan. Anytime you have a Spirit of heaviness, of gloom, of burden, and disgust, Satan is behind it all. Worry and anxiety are also demonic. Learning to recognize these things operating in your life is half the battle, for once you can see them, Satan can no longer continue to work in the dark. When you are aware of what Satan is doing, you will be able to react accordingly. It would also behoove you to learn to resist Satan, because once you do, he will flee. He has no choice. This is a promise laid out in scripture.

If the enemy is operating through the people in your life, it is not unusual for them to display behavior that is out of character for them. They may say and do things that are mean, cruel, hurtful, and inconsiderate. You must be aware of this and not take it personally.

Also, you must not become alarmed or upset when different forms of persecution come your way. If people persecuted Jesus, they will persecute his followers, and you are now one of his followers. Being called a "Jesus freak, being treated like you are an outsider, or being made fun of for your beliefs are not uncommon situations for the people in this stage.

Amidst this persecution is where other Christians are very important. They are a valuable source of encouragement and prayer, and they are extremely effective at helping you to see things more clearly.

In the "Bondage/Egypt" stage, it is not unusual for things to get worse before they get better. It won't be the first time bad things happen, nor will it be the last. Things clearly got worse for the Israelites before they got better. Moses, under the direction of God, went to Egypt to deliver a message from God to the Pharaoh. The message was to let the Israelites go. At that time, the Israelites wanted to go out into the wilderness to worship and honor God for three days (Exodus 5:3). The king's response to Moses was "Well they must not have enough work to do. Stop giving the people straw for making bricks. Make them go and find it for themselves. But still require them to make the same number of bricks as before, not one brick less. They don't have enough work to do, and that is why they keep asking me to let them go and offer sacrifices to their

God!" (Exodus 5:7–8) Their problem got worse not better—they were still under slavery and now they had to work even harder since they were still required to produce the same number of bricks. The Israelites response to this was to get angry with Moses.

If this is happening in your life, that is, if you are under a bondage that appears to be getting worse instead of better, don't worry, it won't change anything. You can still be delivered. The whole idea is that the enemy wants you to take your eyes off of God and to put them on the circumstances surrounding you. This is Satan's way of getting you to take matters into your own hands. He wants your problem to be in your hands, not in God's. From his perspective, you are easier to deal with than the Lord is. Satan can deceive you, but he cannot deceive the Lord. The last thing Satan wants you to do is surrender your problem to the Lord and leave it with Him. The enemy is aware that as long as the problem is in your hands, and as long as you have not learned to trust God yet, that you will not be able to cross over to the Spirit's side of the field. Constant activity on Satan's part is designed to keep you from trusting the Lord.

Many people spend more time than necessary in this stage because they struggle with the process of giving their problem to the Lord. When the Lord begins to work with it, they don't like what He is doing and so they take the problem back. They do this by taking some type of action in an effort to resolve the situation on their own. Often times they do this simply because they think the Lord is taking too long. What they must understand though is that they didn't get into their bondage over night and therefore they more than likely won't get out of it overnight either. James chapter 1 describes a person who does not really trust God to work out a problem. Verses 6–8 say, "But when you pray, you must believe and not doubt at all. Whoever doubts is like a wave in the sea that is driven and blown about by the wind. If you are like that, unable to make up your mind and undecided in all you do, you must not think that you will receive anything from the Lord." You will not get the help you seek if you are unable to let go and let God.

Arriving at the conclusion that you are unable to free yourself from the bondage you're in is an enormous step towards your deliverance. Then, and only then, are you able to give your problem to the Lord and leave it there.

If the problem in your life gets worse, don't despair. Don't panic if you don't understand how God is working things out. His ways are not the same as yours, and usually the way in which He chooses to deliver you from your bondage is not the way you thought He would anyway. Look at the Israelites. Do you honestly believe that they thought that God would open the Red Sea to free them? I'm sure that thought never even crossed their minds.

After a person is saved, does the deception stop? No it does not! Satan is still working (primarily through deceit). It is pretty disconcerting to think that Satan doesn't try to just attack sinners—he works to harm those people who have already turned their lives over to the Lord as well.

Have you ever heard the statement: "Once saved, always saved?" This is deceit. It's a lie and Satan has the Christians fooled with it. The proof that this statement is deceitful lies in the fact that everyone has a free will, and that as long as we have that free will, we can choose to do anything we wish. If we choose to go back to the "Corrupting Forces of the World" stage, we can, but in doing so we relinquish our inheritance. (This is simply the consequences of our actions.) God is not going to allow us to take His Holy Spirit back to the evil that occurs in the lower half of the Spiritual Field. Darkness and light have nothing in common. Taking a look at scripture, we can clearly see that the Lord has already told us that some people will choose to return to the "Corrupting Forces of the World" stage. Look at 2 Peter chapter 2, verses 20–22: "If people have escaped from the corrupting forces of the world through their knowledge of our Lord and Savior Jesus Christ, and then are again caught and conquered by them, such people are in worse condition at the end than they were at the beginning. It would have been much better for them never to have known the way to righteousness than to know it and then turn away from the sacred command that was given to them. What happened to them shows that the proverbs are true: 'A dog goes back to what it has vomited' and 'A pig that has been washed goes back to the mud.'" The pig that has been washed represents the Christian who has been washed clean by the blood of the lamb and has turned and gone back to the mud which is the world. "Once saved always saved" cannot be a true statement as long as we have free will, and since that is something that God will not take away from us, "once saved always saved" is deceit.

Be encouraged. You can and will get through this painful stage by being more focused on what God promises in the Bible and by being more focused on what God is doing as opposed to what Satan is doing.

CHAPTER VI

<u>Deliverance</u>

Although life in the "Bondage/Egypt" stage is mostly painful, it is also filled with many first time experiences and blessings. For the first time in your life, you experience God becoming real to you. For the first time scripture comes alive to you and for the first time a new thirst for God begins in you.

When you are delivered out of the "Bondage/Egypt" stage, it is not just a little deliverance but rather a huge deliverance from something really big that is going on in your life that is causing you to suffer. I have covered several different major types of bondages that are common. Now I must discuss smaller bondages that come as a result of the big ones. For example, for the Israelites, their big bondage was slavery. They spent more than 400 years in this bondage. There is no way that they could have left Egypt and not have resented the Egyptians for what the Egyptians put them through. Resentment was a natural reaction to the type of cruelty that the Israelites endured. When they looked at the scars on their backs from the taskmaster's whip, there is no way that they could not have been bitter.

Common sense tells us that they had every right to be angry too. Resentment, bitterness, and anger are all smaller bondages that came as a result of their big bondage—slavery. When the Israelites crossed over the Red Sea, (which is the fifty-yard line on the diagram), they took these smaller bondages with them. Although they were free from slavery, they still carried with them much resentment, bitterness, and anger. This indicates that it is possible to leave the "Bondage/Egypt" stage, cross over into the "Wilderness" stage, and yet still have some small bondages clinging on. Entrance into the wilderness only represents the absence of the big bondage. Now comes something very different between the "Bondage/Egypt" stage and the "Wilderness" stage. Slavery was something that happened outside of the Israelites. Marital problems are something that happens outside of a person. Bitterness, anger, and resentment, however, are things that happen inside of a person.

In the "Bondage/Egypt" stage, most of the work you see the Lord doing takes place outside of you. Most of this work involves God freeing you from your outside problems. The Israelites saw this in God's dealing with the Egyptians. God sent plagues to Egypt which ultimately helped to free the Israelites from the Egyptians. This is a perfect example of God's hand working in an outside situation to free people. When you move up into the "Wilderness" stage, the work is going to be done inside of you.

It is not uncommon for people to mistake these two different types of bondages for each other. It is sometimes easy to mistake the smaller bondage (that is actually a result of the big bondage) for the big one. For example, take a person who has an addiction to alcohol. For one person this may be the big bondage, for another it may be the result of something much deeper that is manifesting itself through the addiction to alcohol. In this case, it is possible for a person to receive deliverance from an interior bondage while still in the "Bondage/Egypt" stage, because it is interfering with his spiritual growth. In the case of alcohol, for example, how can a person ever grow spiritually if he cannot remember anything? The Lord couldn't wait until the person got to the "Wilderness" stage to deal with it because otherwise that person would never make it.

Deliverance is not something that you provide for yourself but rather is something that God has to provide for you. Once this occurs, you will experience great joy. You will be happier than you've been in a long time. It is also common to experience a spiritual high at this time.

In learning about the Journey, many people want to know just how long they have to stay in this "Bondage/Egypt" stage. This is something that no one can tell them. The length of time each person spends in this stage varies. The only thing that is known for sure is that up until this point, the person has spent most of his life somewhere in the "Corrupting Forces of the World" stage.

The point of deliverance is represented by the fifty-yard line (see illustration). This is the dividing line. It can also be called the "Red Sea Experience." It indicates God's direct intervention in your personal life to free you from the bondage you have been living in. God intervened in the personal lives of the Israelites in order to free them (see Exodus 3:9–10), and He did the same thing in St. Paul's life (see Acts 9:3).

Deliverance is usually quick. You may spend several years in the "Bondage/Egypt" stage, but on the dawn of your deliverance, you can expect to be freed quickly. This should offer hope to those of you who know that you are currently in the "Bondage/Egypt" stage.

As mentioned previously, the Israelites spent over 400 years in the "Bondage/Egypt" stage. However, on the dawn of their deliverance the Lord said "Get up and go." The Egyptians pursued them to the Red Sea, at which time Moses told them "Don't be afraid! Stand your ground, and you will see what the Lord will do to save you today; you will never see these Egyptians again. The Lord will fight for you, and all you have to do is keep still" (Exodus 14:13–14).

There are several messages in this for

every single Christian on the planet. First, when it is time for you to be delivered, you will not be required to do anything but trust and obey what the Lord is telling you. He will do everything else that is required to free you. Nothing the Israelites said or did freed them. It was God who freed them. The only requirement was that they trust Him, and do what He instructed them to do through Moses. On the day of your deliverance, you will sense that God wants you to do something. When this happens, you must not hesitate, but rather get up and do whatever He tells you to do. Until you are able to accomplish trusting God and being obedient to Him you will remain in bondage.

The second message is that when God delivers you, it will be life changing. It will be the very thing that will move you up into the next stage.

The third message is that when you are delivered from your bondage, you must continue to move forward. Those Israelites who left Egypt with Moses and then wanted to return to Egypt made God angry! You will do well to keep this in mind.

CHAPTER VII

THE WILDERNESS

Level I: Entry into the Wilderness

Congratulations, you are now on the Spirit's side of the field! Life among the people here is much more serene. In the early part of the "Wilderness" stage, you won't experience too much trouble from the enemy. However, rest assured that he is not happy that you have succeeded in crossing over to the next stage—this means he failed at stopping you. Instead of giving up on defeating you, he will simply go back and re-group. He now has to come up with a new plan of attack since the ways in which he works in the lives of Christians on this side of the field is entirely different from the ways he works in the lives of sinners on the other side of the field.

Experiencing deliverance will be the biggest step you take on your entire Journey. When you arrive at this point it is very common for you to get a rest. (If those of you who have already been through this area of the Journey will think back, you will recall that the rest was there.) This rest feels so good because you have just gone through that turbulent time in your life where

God was gently trying to draw you into a personal relationship with Him and Satan was trying to keep you right in the midst of the chaos on his side of the field. You also had all the activity associated with your big bondage as well. For a long time, your life was very chaotic and painful. By the time you arrive in the "Wilderness" stage you might not even be able to remember the last time your life was so peaceful and quiet.

This rest is very needed at this time. However, a lot of people struggle with the Lord at this point. They have become so accustomed to all the activity associated with the big bondage, that when everything becomes quiet they do not know what to do with themselves. Now that the pain is gone, they want to go on with the business of serving the Lord. They think they are ready to start serving, but they are not ready yet. This is because they do not yet know enough to minister to others. It is crucial for everyone to understand that God intends for you to take the rest and enjoy it.

Consider the Israelites again. Shortly after they crossed over the Red Sea, God led them to an oasis in the desert. There were twelve springs and seventy palm trees (Exodus 15:27). It was here that they were able to rest following their long journey from Egypt. When you reach this rest area, you might as well enjoy it because you will be spending quite some time here.

Once you cross over into the "Wilderness"

stage, you will quickly see that things are entirely different from anything you have experienced before. You will notice that things are much more serene and quieter among the people residing in God's territory. There is an absence of stress and tension, and a sense of well-being. You will feel the Lord's presence. Scripture reading and prayer should have become a regular part of your everyday life by now. This is one of the times in the Journey when it will be easy to praise God for everything He has done for you. Gratitude will be foremost in your heart.

Those around you will notice something different about you. They will not be able to put their finger on it, but they will watch you carefully, usually saying nothing. You will begin to find yourself uncomfortable around evil—the same type of evil that you once lived among back in the "Corrupting Forces of the World" stage. For many Christians, it is also common to feel very dependent on the Lord at this point.

It is not unusual for people here not to be attached to a prayer group or community at this time. God wants you to rest and be peaceful and calm. Read your scriptures and pray. This is all He wants you to do right now. From this time until the end of the Journey, there will be times when the Lord will pull you out of the mainstream of activity and tell you to rest. If you struggle against this rest, you will be outside the will of God. Spiritual rest either precedes something big happening or it follows it. Deliverance is something big.

Along with this rest, you will also receive another test. This will be God testing you to see if you are going to be obedient. There will be nothing painful happening in your life. This does not mean that there will not be things happening that you do not like, but any bad things you experience now will be small in comparison to what you have just come through.

Level 11: Beginning a Ministry

How will you know when the rest period is over and it is time to move on? You will know this when your ministry begins. Seldom do true Spirit-filled ministries start before this point. Why? Well in order to begin a true Spirit-filled ministry, you first need to have accepted the Lord as your personal Savior so at least you are going in the right direction. Second, you need to have experienced the baptism in the spirit because that's where you get the power needed to minister effectively. (The Holy Spirit is not going to work through you if you don't have Him in you.) Third, you will need to have been delivered from your bondage so that you can take your eyes off yourself and put them on someone else. All these things happen before you cross over to the Spirit's side of the field. If you have not experienced these things, you should not be ministering to anyone. Therefore, a true spirit-filled ministry does not start until you have reached this point in your Journey.

The way in which the Lord begins to show you that it is time to begin your ministry will be clear to you. He will start to form the circumstances in your life that will put you in the place where he wishes for you to serve.

Much of God's will for your life is hidden in the circumstance of your life. For example, if you are married and have several children at home, it is pretty safe to say that God is not going to ask you to leave your family and go to Siberia to minister. God intends for the family unit to be together. If you already have an obligation and responsibility that comes with a family, your ministry will not interfere with it.

I remember very clearly when God revealed His plan of ministry in my life. At the time, I had no idea that God was behind the series of events that took place. My husband was in the military services. We had already spent a number of years overseas and had just returned to the United States approximately six months earlier. One day my husband called to inform me that once again, he had orders to go back overseas. The assignment was for England. Had I stopped and thought about it, I would have known that there was something out of the ordinary happening. People do not usually receive orders that quickly. I, however, did not think about that. Instead I screamed "I refuse to go back overseas!

Uncle Sam owns you not me! Forget it!" I was truly upset! In an effort to calm me down, my husband offered to go through the proper channels to find out if he could get out of this assignment. He, too, thought it was a mistake and that he probably had a very strong chance of being released from the assignment. He called the office that was responsible for issuing orders, but couldn't get through. He tried numerous times a day for several days and still could not get through.

In the meantime, the Lord had begun to work on me. I began to sense that the military really was not responsible for this, God was. So when I spoke to my husband, I told him, "Let's not be too hasty, this just might be the Lord!" Needless to say, he was shocked by my sudden change of heart. I quickly informed him to not get too excited, because if I could stay in the will of God and not go I would rather do that. So together we sought the will of God through prayer.

It soon became clear that the Lord was already beginning to form the circumstances in our lives to put us into the place where he wanted us to minister. It didn't take much time in prayer for us to realize that it really was the Lord behind it all. So, I had a choice. I could choose not to go and live outside of what I felt for sure was the will of God for my life, or I could choose to go, and follow God's plan for my life. I had the choice of obeying God or not. There is something about me that will not allow me to deliberately disobey

God. I know that one cannot receive the blessing of God if he is operating outside of His will. So in my prayer time, I relented and told the Lord that I would go. Since He can read my heart, He knew that I was making a choice to be obedient even though it went totally against my desires.

I did, however, have a few requests of my own. Since it would be in the middle of January when we would arrive at the new base, I asked the Lord to go before us and prepare a place for us to live. I also requested a community with a good Christian church and a prayer group. Next was the matter of the children. We had three. They would have to change schools in the middle of winter, and probably would be resentful at having to make a move and leave their friends. Since we had made overseas moves before, I knew how the move would really disrupt the children's lives. I knew that adjusting to a new life that was completely different from what they had been accustomed to would be difficult so I prayed for the Lord to make the move go as smoothly as possible.

Eventually it was time to go and we all left very reluctantly. The problems with the move began immediately, and we were disappointed in the new base from the beginning. The base was very small and had only the minimum of facilities operating. We had arrived late in the evening, and were all tired and hungry. Much to our surprise, there were no restaurants open. We were told that we should go to the Mini-Mart and purchase something to take back to the hotel to cook. After the long exhausting trip overseas with three children, the last thing I wanted to do was cook. On top of all this, the baby was sick with an ear infection. We had taken him to the doctor just prior to leaving the United States, and we were given penicillin to administer to him. What we didn't know was that he was allergic to penicillin. If you have ever seen a person have a reaction to penicillin it is frightening, especially a baby. Not surprising, there was no hospital at the new base either, just a small clinic. My husband called the clinic to find out what to do. He was told that since the baby was not an active duty person, he would have to take him to another base located two hours away. The clinic could only treat non-active duty people during regular duty hours. Obviously, it was not possible to take our son to the other base. We had no car, didn't know where it was, and knew no one. We ended up staying up all night with him. When it was time to give him another dose of penicillin, something told me not to administer it. I thank God every day for guiding me and warning me not to give him that next dose.

Early the next morning, my husband wrapped the baby in a blanket and walked to the clinic in the bone-chilling cold, stopping people along the way for directions. The medical personnel at the clinic told my husband that our son was having a severe allergic reaction to the penicillin.

First impressions have a powerful effect, and our first impression of this base was that we were obviously being punished for something. The whole experience was completely disgusting to us; unfortunately, there was no way out of the situation at that point.

After only a few days, military regulation required that my husband begin to process into the base. This left my children and I to find something to occupy our time. It didn't take long before I got bored and decided to go shopping. There was only one place to shop on the base. When I walked in the door of the Base Exchange, I saw a little lady, an employee, standing by a display case stocking greeting cards. I had never seen her before. She looked up at me and immediately stopped. I noticed that she was staring at me. I continued to walk down the aisle and turned around to find that she was still staring. She just wouldn't take her eyes off me. I wondered if she had been in this God forsaken place for so long that she had lost all contact with reality. I couldn't figure out whether she was just plain rude or curious.

Finally, she walked up and said, "You're the one." I looked at her trying to figure out what she was talking about, all the while thinking that she was really strange. She went on to say, "I'm so sorry, I must apologize for staring at you. My husband and I are committed Christians and it's about time for us to return to the United States. But there is no one here to take our place and carry on the Word of God. We have been praying to the Lord to let us know without a shadow of a doubt whether or not we should extend our tour and stay until he sent someone, or whether we should leave. As you walked in the door, there was something over you. I knew in my Spirit, that you were the one God had sent."

Frankly, I was puzzled and had no idea what "You're the one" meant, nor did I have any idea what I was supposed to do with the information the woman had shared with me. I finished my shopping and returned to the hotel pondering this whole incident over in my mind.

In the meantime, we had to find a place to live, and I reminded the Lord that I had already asked Him to go before us and prepare a place, and I was counting on him to do it. The problem was that the place He found was approximately fifty miles one way from the base. The housing area was located on top of a hill surrounded by cows and sheep. Not only that, it was a little cracker-jack box of a house that hadn't been lived in for forty years.

When we went to look at the house, I immediately told my husband that there was no way I was going to live in that house. He agreed with me. We returned to the base and turned the house down saying that it was unfit for human habitation.

The location of the house was also a big concern. There was no commissary, no post office, no restaurants, no recreational facilities, no library, and no stores. There was nothing one would expect to be within a reasonable distance from their home. All the area had to offer besides housing was one gas pump, a small school, and a Mini-Mart. For everything else needed, you were expected to drive 100 miles (round trip) to the base.

Meanwhile, as I was having my regular prayer time, I began to wonder if the Lord had some more surprises in store for us. Finally, the Lord said to me, "I didn't promise you a mansion on earth. I promised you a roof over your head. Is that not a roof?" My reply, "Barely Lord, but it is a roof." All the prayers, pleading, and rationalizing with the Lord did not alter the strong sense that this was indeed the house that the Lord had for us. So we reluctantly moved into the house.

As bad as this was, we were unaware at the time that this was not to be our biggest disappointment. In my prayer time I again asked the Lord a number of questions. Like everyone else who is in this part of the Journey, my relationship with the Lord was paramount to me. There were certain things that I expected to be available to me when we moved into the house. One of these things was a nearby church. So I asked the Lord to lead me to the church that He wanted us to attend. His reply, "There is no church." "What about a prayer group?" I asked. "There is no prayer group," said the Lord. At that point I was starting to become desperate as I thought about how I was going to survive spiritually. "Lord," I said, "just one more question please. Where are the Christians?" "There are no Christians," was His reply. The nearest Christians were at least a hundred miles away at the base. We were part of an influx of new personnel being assigned to this base, and since the base was very small, the housing area was located far from the base. At this point, I threw the biggest spiritual fit known to man. Never in my wildest dreams, would it have occurred to me that the Lord would do something like this!

This was to be my home for the next three years. In my prayer time, I cried, I pleaded, and I begged the Lord to change the circumstances of my life. As you can see, there is still a lot of self-ishness in a person who is in this level of the "Wilderness" stage. I was still feeding the flesh in me. And at that point my flesh was not very happy with anything. I had not grown to the place where the things of the flesh no longer mattered to me. I wanted everything that I was accustomed to and felt entitled to.

Finally, I surrendered myself to the situation and asked the Lord for just one more favor. I asked Him to allow me to grow spiritually in spite of the odds against doing so. God's ways and our ways are truly different. Never in a million years could I have imagined what God had in store for us.

Shortly after this time, my husband and I both began to sense in our spirits that God wanted us to start a church. This was a definite sign that our ministry was about to begin. Not only had the Lord put us in the place where He wanted us to minister, it was very clear that there was a dire need for something spiritual in this place. The assignment that the Lord gave us was apostleship. That sounds like something really big, but all it means is that the Lord chooses a person or persons to go into an area to advocate a change. We were just the vessels; it was God who brought about the change.

The first thing He wanted us to do was to start a church. "But Lord, I said, there is no building, there are no chairs, there's no altar, there isn't even a priest up here." I clearly thought I did not understand Him correctly, and that this had to be a mistake! I continued to say to the Lord: "There are not even any people up here who act like church is important to them." His reply: "If you listen to me and follow the directions of my Holy Spirit, there will be a church." At that time, I wasn't really accustomed to the Lord communicating with me in that way—most of the time it was like I just knew what He wanted done and when He wanted me to do it.

Needless to say, my husband and I were both very scared and felt totally inadequate to take on a project of such magnitude. At that point I could really understand how Moses must have felt when he was given the responsibility of leading the Israelites out of the land of Egypt. Following the Lord's will can be frightening, but rest assured He will lead you every step of the way.

Another point that bears mentioning is that by this point on the field, you will have grown enough to listen to the Lord. God communicates His instructions to His people through various methods. He may use scripture, a good Christian book, another Christian, a minister or pastor, thoughts planted in your mind, or He may grant you a particular sense of what He wishes for you to do. By this point you will have also grown enough to see what God's will is for you through different events in your life. Having passed through the "Bondage/Egypt" stage, your faith will have grown too. You will have witnessed first-hand what God will do *for* His people and now is the time for God to show you what He will do *through* His people.

In getting the church off the ground, we had to deal with people in positions of power on the base. On any military installation, nothing of significance can happen without the knowledge and approval of the Base Commander. However, in this case, it had to go even higher to headquarters. The message came down from headquarters that there would be no church. According to headquarters, if the people wanted to go to church, they would have to drive over one hundred miles round trip to the base. I knew that the people were not going to do that. They already had to drive that distance five days a week to go to work, and on Saturday to get necessities. They simply were not going to drive that far on Sundays to go to church.

It is true that the Holy Spirit works in mysterious ways. The people who were in the positions to stop this project suddenly were re-assigned to other bases and were replaced by new people who were much more receptive and cooperative.

We followed the Lord's directions, and as He said, the church was born. Many people who had not been to church for years, began to come back. Little children who had not received their baptisms got baptized. These were the fruits. All spirit-filled ministries will produce fruits. Clearly, these fruits are out of the control of the person who is ministering. No matter how hard we worked, we could not touch the hearts of the people and make them desire to come to church. It was only the Lord who was able to do that.

In the meantime, without our being aware of it, we were being watched very carefully by members of other religious denominations. Praise the Lord! It wasn't long before services were being held for them as well. It was truly an incredible experience and life up on the hill was beginning to look a lot brighter.

After the church was off and running, my husband and I began to sense again that we were to do something else; but we had no idea what it was. Like everyone else, we had to wait until the Lord revealed to us what he wished us to do. Then one day in prayer, it became clear to me that our next assignment was to start a religious education program. We, along with other members of the congregation, got into our cars and went to other bases in the country and requested that they donate to us any religious books that they no longer needed. God blessed our efforts and the religious education program began two months later.

God in his loving kindness placed many good people in our lives to help with all the work that needed to be accomplished. They became as committed in doing the Lord's work as we were. One couple became so involved and helped in so many different ways, that they became an integral part of everything that was happening. Others donated enormous time, talents, and energy to make sure that everything went smoothly. I will always praise the Lord for having allowed us to meet such wonderful, spirit-filled people. As an extra benefit, many of these people and their families have remained our good friends for years, even though we live in different parts of the United States now.

Following the initiation of the religious education program, a bible study was also born.

I felt totally ill-equipped to lead such a group. I had never been in that type of position before. I had always attended bible studies, but I had never led one. Again, my fears of not being capable of effectively conducting a weekly study surfaced.

Next came the second ministry to which I had been called. The first had been apostleship for both my husband and I but the second one was only for me. Through the circumstances of my life and prayer time, it became clear to me that the Lord wanted me to teach.

For years I had been studying scripture. It wasn't something that was foreign to me, but again I had to look for the fruits of the Spirit. If there were no fruits to be seen from my labor, then I would know without a doubt that this was not what the Lord wanted of me at that time. In this case however, as word spread throughout the military family housing area, people began to come. They started to study the bible—something that many of them had never done. People began to invite the Lord into their hearts and some even received the baptism of the spirit. These were the fruits! God blessed this group abundantly, and they were really bound together with the love of God. This was something no human being could have done; it had to have come from the Lord himself.

Hopefully my sharing these events with you allows you to clearly see how God formed the circumstances in the lives of my husband and I that put us in the place of ministry. Once God got us in this place, He began to reveal to us exactly what He wished for us to do.

Before your ministry begins, you will have to exercise some faith. For example, if God is going to bestow on you the gift of healing, you will have to exercise some faith by believing that God is still in the business of healing and that God will work through you. If the gift is prophecy, you have to also exercise faith by opening your mouth and speaking forth God's message. Faith is the key here, no matter what the gift or ministry is.

A ministry in its basic terms is your area of service, which God has already prepared for you. The first step in any successful ministry is to come to the realization that it is never you who is responsible for accomplishing anything. You are simply the vessel through which the power of the Holy Spirit works. You cannot have a powerful ministry without faith, holy fear of God, and true devotion to Christ. All three are essential. The Bible says that we are to offer ourselves as living sacrifices, dedicated to His service (Romans 12:1). Dedication does not mean that you should do the ministry when you feel like it. It means you must be committed to do what God requires of you whenever He leads you to do it.

Proverbs chapter 9, verse 10 says, "The fear of the Lord is the beginning of wisdom, and the knowledge of the Holy One is understanding." Knowledge and understanding are the basis of ministry and both are tied into the Lord. An effective minister will never forget this. Staying in union with Christ yourself is the only way you can continue to minister effectively, because without Him, you can do nothing. A steady diet of scripture reading and quiet time with Christ is a necessity. The more time you spend with the Lord, the more effective you are going to be in your ministry. The Word of God says that the Holy Spirit will teach you everything you need to know (1 John 2:27). Depend on Him to teach you how to minister properly and effectively.

There are nine gifts of the Holy Spirit listed in 1Corinthians chapter 12. They are given to build up the church. The first gift is wisdom. Anyone can ask for this gift. It is valuable to you in any ministry that you receive. The second gift is knowledge, but this one comes with a warning. The Bible clearly says that if you claim to have this gift and you do not, the consequences will be that you will lose your way to faith (1Timothy 6:20–21). Therefore you must be really careful with claiming to have this gift. The third gift is faith. If you feel you do not have enough faith, you should ask the Lord to help the little faith that you do have to grow. The more faith you have, the more powerfully the Lord can use you in His service. The fourth gift is healing. This is a beautiful gift but it is one that has a tendency to cause a person to feel more special than those who have the other gifts. No one gift is more important then any of the others. They are all needed. Those who are blessed with this gift need to remember to always give the glory to God. After all, it is He who performs the actual healing anyway. Miracles are the next gift mentioned in scripture. This doesn't need an explanation. Yes, it is true that God is indeed still in the business of performing miracles through His appointed servants. Proclaiming God's message is another gift mentioned in 1 Corinthians chapter 12. This gift involves announcing publicly what God is telling you privately. In scripture, we see this gift exercised through John the Baptist, Jeremiah, Jonah, St. Paul, and many others. The next gift is discernment. This is the gift that allows a person to tell when a message comes from God or when it comes from another source. It is in your best interest to ask the Lord in prayer to grant you this gift. Speaking in tongues and interpretation of tongues are additional gifts. They are two entirely different things. Lots of people can speak in tongues, but few can interpret what is being said.

You cannot have any gift of the Spirit without first receiving the baptism in the spirit. The Holy Spirit does not operate through you if you do not have Him in you. Everyone who receives the baptism in the Spirit will receive a gift. You should know that the Holy Spirit gives a different gift to each person (1 Corinthians 12:11).

This is Level II of the "Wilderness" stage. It begins with God forming the circumstances in which you will be ministering. Most of what is happening in this level has to do with your ministry.

There is another thing about ministries that is important to mention. This is something that I have found to be true in my own life as well as in the lives of other Christians. The Lord might decide to empower you in a moment to use you as a vessel to operate in a gift for something that needs to be done at a certain time, but then not allow you to keep that gift. Let me explain this. If, for example you are a willing vessel of the Lord, and you happen to be available when God wants to say something to someone, He may decide to use you to do it. This happened to me with the gift of prophecy.

One hot, summer night in 1981 in the Philippines, without warning, God's anointing came over me and the prophecy began. My husband and I were in our car. We were about to make a very important decision that was going to affect the rest of our lives. I was getting ready to return to the states with the children. He was going to remain overseas. I was in the "Bondage/Egypt" stage. The prophetic message I received instructed us on what the Lord intended to do in our lives. A split second before this, the Lord told me that He was going to put into my mouth the words He wanted me to speak. As soon as He said this, I received an even stronger anointing and the prophetic message began. It lasted twenty minutes. I used to wonder when I was reading scripture how the prophets of old were able to stake their lives on the messages they received. After I experienced this, I understood. It was unmistakable. For one thing, the order was reversed, meaning that I wasn't thinking first and then speaking. I was speaking and then thinking about what was being revealed. I, too, could stake my life on what that message said. The prophecy did not come true for two years, but it did happen. The Lord did not use me again in that way for another four years. Although this is a wonderful gift, it is not one that seems to be with me all the time.

There is, however, one gift that will be with you all the time and that gift is different for each person. For example, my gift is speaking in tongues and my husband's gift is faith. This gift is to be used in your area of service. God does not send His people out ill-equipped. Whatever your ministry is, you will have everything you need in order to function effectively.

When your ministry begins, you will have reached Level II of the Wilderness. It does not mean that this will be the only thing that will be going on in your spiritual life, but it will be the predominant thing.

LEVEL III: LEARNING TO WALK BY FAITH

You have been traveling in the "Wilderness" stage for quite some time by the time you've made it through the first two levels. However, now is the time to go deeper into the "Wilderness" experience. So how do you know when it is time to move on to the next level of the "Wilderness" stage? You will know when God creates the circumstances in your life that will take you out of your ministry and put you on the shelf so to speak. In other words, you will not have an assignment from the Lord.

For me, this proved to be a very painful experience because I was unwilling to let go. I thoroughly enjoyed the ministry that the Lord had bestowed on me. Therefore, God had to allow a number of painful events to happen to force me to let go.

My heart's desire was to continue to teach and lead prayer meetings and bible studies. I had become very comfortable in that position and desperately wanted to continue after we left England. That, however, was not God's plan for me. There is a big difference in serving God the way He wishes to be served and serving Him the way we want to serve. In hindsight, I now realize that I simply didn't want to move on. I was like a person in his senior year of high school who loved every minute of it so much that he refused to move on and accept the fact that it was time for him to go to college. Yes, that was immature, but it was certainly the way I felt at the time. I wanted to continue to serve Him the way I wanted to. He, on the other hand, was ready to do some major interior work in me.

The third level of the "Wilderness" stage carries with it some very distinct symptoms that set it apart from the other levels. Here is where the interior work really gets underway.

The "Wilderness" stage is the longest stage in the entire Journey. You will spend more time here than you will in any other stage. The length of time spent here varies. It depends on the person. It depends on how quickly you are able to surrender control of everything in your life to the Lord and how cooperative you are with the Lord's plan for you.

There is much that is going to be happening to you in this stage. Most of the interior work that needs to be accomplished will occur at this point in the Journey. God will not give you more than you can handle, so the process is sometimes very slow.

One of the first things that will happen when you reach Level III of the "Wilderness" stage is that you will begin to experience some confusion in your interior life. This confusion is fairly mild in the beginning but becomes more pronounced as you continue to travel down the path God has chosen for you. There will be fewer people on the road then there was in the other stages of the Journey. Therefore, meeting someone who is at least this far in the Journey will be rare. Consider it a blessing if you are privileged enough to find someone at your same level at this point in your life. For the most part, you will walk alone with the Lord for awhile.

Another characteristic of this level is that the presence of God doesn't seem to be there anymore. You will be doing the same things you have always done in your prayer time, but there is nothing but silence from the Lord. A lot of people will do prayer group hopping at this time, in effort to hang on to the feeling of closeness they once had with the Lord. God doesn't want you to do that. He wants you to keep moving on towards the goal, which is the "Jesus Stage" (see illustration). Herein lays one of the biggest differences between the "Bondage/Egypt" stage and the "Wilderness" stage.

In the "Wilderness" stage, you are required to walk by faith. This was not so in the "Bondage/Egypt" stage, since the people there usually do not have the kind of faith that allows them to stand on the Word of God and believe simply because God said it. God does not require anyone to give more than they are able. This is why from the time you left the "Bondage/Egypt" stage until you reached this level of the "Wilderness" stage, the Lord has been quietly working deep within you. There is a gradual spiritual growth process that occurs which will make you capable of walking by faith. Most people are not aware of this process when it is happening.

In this stage of the "Wilderness," you can expect the joy you once felt to be gone most of the time. In fact, the joy will be few and far between for a long time.

Having an extremely hard time praying and reading scripture is also normal at this time. When this happens, it does not mean you are backsliding. It's easy to read scripture and pray when you feel like it and when you feel warm and nourished after doing so. It becomes very difficult to read and pray in the "Wilderness" stage though because God is no longer feeding your feelings. He is developing your faith. It will require determination and a deliberate act of your will to succeed in continuing your regular quiet time with the Lord. There will be no more joy in doing it now. You are required to read scripture because you know you should, not because you will feel anything. If you are experiencing these characteristics, you are in Level III of the "Wilderness" stage. The major lesson is to learn to walk by faith.

At this point in my spiritual life, something strange began to happen in me. I came to the realization that I was not happy. I knew that I could not find happiness in the world and what it had to offer, but I wasn't elated with the things of God anymore either. This is not unusual since God is no longer feeding your feelings.

By now, my love for the Lord had grown and I knew in my heart that I simply could not walk away from Him. As frustrating as this level was, I could not just throw up my hands and quit. I knew that His way was the right way and that any selfish action on my part would place me outside of His will. It took a long time for me to realize that I was being tested to see if I was going to remain faithful in spite of the difficulties that came along with this stage.

LEVEL IV: BATTLING THE FLESH

Level IV will take you even deeper into the "Wilderness" experience. There are several signs that will let you know that you have reached this point. Profound confusion is a definite sign. This is normal and occurs in every Christian's walk. The reason this is happening is that the deep purification, purging, and cleansing have begun. Here the real struggle begins. Conviction is another sign that you have reached Level IV of the "Wilderness" stage. You will start to experience conviction in regard to things that you know are not right, but that your flesh wants to do anyway. The result is that you will have a fierce interior struggle going on. Your spirit will want to do that which is right, but you will struggle with your flesh. The flesh, also known as the self, is that part of a person that is sinful. In the Gospel of

Matthew, there is a conversation between Jesus and Peter where Jesus actually tells Peter that his flesh is weak (Matthew 26:41). Going through this level of the Journey, you will clearly be able to identify; with Jesus' statement to Peter, because you will see that we are exactly the same way. You will discover that all of us have weaknesses of the flesh. That is why it is extremely important to consider your prayer time as a necessity. You will definitely need the grace of God to get through this level.

LEVEL V: PUSHING THROUGH TROUBLE VALLEY

Level V of the "Wilderness" stage will introduce you to "Trouble Valley." It is a world all of its own. It is sometimes called the dark night. It has also been referred to as the death of self. It is a period of excessive dryness. "Trouble Valley" derives its name from the turmoil you are going to feel inside when you go through it. It is a long and painful stage. A lot of the transformation in your life is going to take place here. The first thing God will do is to take the blinders off your eyes. He will then allow you to see yourself as you really are. This process is not done all at once, but rather gradually because God will not give you more than you can handle.

You will begin to see your "flesh," the sin that lives in you, as a problem that impedes your relationship with the Lord. You will begin to see how sinful you really are. God will often show you this by allowing you to see how sinful your actions and reactions are to the situations in your life.

In Level V of the "Wilderness" stage, you will become acutely aware that you are not holy. You will realize that you have a long way to go. You will see that the self in you really has to die if you are going to succeed.

The "Wilderness" stage is tough. You will not be able to compare your walk with anyone else. The length of time each person spends here varies. Although it will not seem like it to you, most of the interior transformation is occurring— God is just doing it gradually. Since the "Wilderness" experience is so long, it is not uncommon for people to literally die while still going through it. However, it is not impossible to successfully get through this level in your life-time. Taking a look at scripture, we see that Joshua did. He left Egypt with the Israelites and it was he that led them into the Promised Land. Joshua became Moses successor, and if you read in Deuteronomy chapter 31, verses 7–8, you will see where Joshua is commissioned by Moses to take his place. It reads: "Then Moses called Joshua and said to him in the presence of all the people of Israel, 'Be determined and confident; you are the one who will lead these people to occupy the land that the Lord promised to their ancestors. The Lord himself will lead you and be with you. He will not fail you or abandon you, so do not lose courage or be afraid.'" Obviously

Joshua was not the only one who left Egypt and entered the Promised Land. Some of the people he led also left Egypt when he did. This all happened while Joshua was still going through his own "Wilderness" experience.

In Matthew chapter 7, verses 13–14, scripture says, "Go in through the narrow gate, because the gate to hell is wide and the road that leads to it is easy, and there are many who travel it. But the gate to life is narrow and the way that leads to it is hard, and there are few people who find it." The further you go through the Journey, the fewer people you will encounter. However, if you persevere, God will grant you entrance into the Promised Land. If you are called home to the Lord before you complete this part of the Journey, don't worry, you will be in God's hands and He will see that you enter the gates of Heaven. For those who wish to make it into the Promised Land, they can get a lot accomplished here on earth if only they will allow the Lord to work in them and through them.

One should understand that much of the lessons to be learned here cannot be learned in heaven. For example, long suffering is a fruit of the spirit that is developed in you. The only way to acquire this particular fruit is to suffer a long time. That can't be accomplished in heaven since there is no suffering there. Many of the lessons we learn throughout our lives are learned as a result of some type of difficulty. Revelation 21:4 tells us that in heaven, there will be no more grief, no more crying, and no more pain. There is no circumstance in heaven that will produce the Fruits of the Spirit in us; therefore, we must have these qualities prior to our entrance into heaven.

God sometimes teaches us lessons through physical pain as well. Obviously, these are more lessons which cannot be acquired in heaven since no one there is in any pain at all. It behooves each of us to understand this basic truth. To become one of God's saints you will suffer. No student is greater than his master. Jesus suffered and so will His followers. If you cooperate with the Holy Spirit, He will see to it that you will not be wasting precious time granted you on earth.

During our look at the Israelites journey, we saw that many of them died in the Wilderness. On one occasion, three thousand died in one day (Exodus 32:25–29). In much the same way, it is not uncommon for people in these latter days to pass away while still in the Wilderness.

Complaining is something that is quite common for the people who are at this point of the Journey. Although it is not something that God wants us to do, the Israelites did it in the Wilderness, (Exodus 16:2–12), and not surprisingly, many modern day Christians do it as well. The fact that you feel that there is something worth complaining about is an indication that you are not happy with your life at this time. Since the cleansing, purging, and purification process is ongoing, you will find yourself in many situations that you do not like. For example, if you have a problem with pride, God will want to purge you of it. Hence, you will find yourself in many situations where you will be humiliated and put to shame. If you are impatient, look for the Lord to allow you to be placed in situations where patience is required. Obviously, no one wants to be humiliated and placed in stressful situations, but the fact that you are going to be unhappy with some of the things that are happening to you is to be expected. You can count on the Lord to put anything that is not of God in you under a spotlight and deal with it.

For most people, anger will be the most common emotion they will experience. As a warning, you should not take yourself out of situations in your life that anger you since God has allowed these for your purification. Should you choose to remove yourself from such a situation, you can expect to find yourself in a similar one later on that will no doubt require you to learn the same lesson that God intended for you to learn the first time around.

During this level of the Journey, you will also be called to exercise self-discipline. Self-discipline tends to be a stumbling block because the self in us has an insatiable appetite for wanting its own way. Another hindrance is gluttony. Most of us who are able to be honest with ourselves realize that we are guilty of some form of this sin. For most of our lives we have been over-feeding the self and indulging in the things that please it. Therefore, gluttony must be dealt with, and self-discipline will be required. This is not easy, but certainly necessary.

Since this area of the Journey is so painful, it is not uncommon for people to feel that their lives are out of control during this process. You must ask yourself, "Is my life truly out of control or is it just not going the way I wish?" If you feel that your life is out of control, then the self in you is still quite alive and well, since dead things do not feel. In the spiritual sense, when you try to practice self-discipline, it is the self in you that thinks everything in your life is out of control; for it makes no sense to the self to deprive itself of the things it sees will bring it happiness, contentment, and pleasure.

Do not look for the Lord to pamper you in this level. A pampered person is one who is unbroken, self-centered, and useless to God. This kind of person is unable to see beyond himself nor is he able to deny himself for the good of the kingdom. The things necessary in spiritual growth are the very things viewed by a pampered, self-centered person as something to be avoided at all cost. Suffering, sacrifice, obedience, self-denial, and discipline are all foreign to this type of person. A lifetime of indulging in self-worship creates a person who is in great need of divine work in order to prepare him for what lies ahead.

Level VI: Becoming a New Creation

The task that needs to be accomplished by the Lord at this level is to make us the new creation He promised we would become. He never said He was going to fix the old self in us. Ephesians chapter 4, verses 22–24 say "So get rid of your old self, which made you live as you used to—the old self that was being destroyed by its deceitful desires. Your hearts and minds must be made completely new, and you must put on the new self, which is created in God's likeness and reveals itself in the true life that is upright and holy." The Lord also must mold us into people who are productive. This cannot be accomplished but by afflictions, trials, discipline, suffering, and tribulations; none of which are things that the self is going to like. You can expect all these things to become a regular part of your life until the purification in you is completed.

One of the most enduring lessons I have learned in my life came one day in my quiet time when the Lord gave me some insight into the area of afflictions. Afflictions are pressures or anything that causes you distress and suffering. When afflictions are allowed in a Christian's life, there is always a lesson to be learned. Many of God's people fail to see the lesson because they spend too much time focusing on the affliction itself. Afflictions are to be endured quietly, calmly, and with faith and trust in God. Complaining, resisting, rebelling, or giving oneself over to depression and despair are all evidence of lack of trust in God and are indications that more deep interior work needs to be accomplished. You must place yourself solely into His hands. For He who made you will make all things work together for your good. The sting of each affliction will soon ease as you begin to see the Lord in all things.

Through the purification process, you will begin to discover that you are actually becoming more Christ-like. You will be able to put other's needs before your own. You will become capable of praying for people who have hurt you, and in some cases have continued to hurt you. Turning the other cheek and praying for those who despitefully use you are all indications that the interior work being done in you is successful. In short, you will be capable of being the kind of person that scripture tells you to be, but which up to this point in your life have been unable to be no matter how hard you tried. The process is so gradual, that often we are not aware that a change has taken place until the Lord places us in certain situations and we discover that our reactions are different than they were before.

Scripture reading continues to be difficult at this time. The words of the Bible might become confusing to you, or you may not remember what you have read. We get our nourishment from scripture, and though prayer we communicate with God, but the frustration we feel trying to remain faithful in our prayer time will cause us to struggle. Anything worth having is worth struggling for. You can depend on the Lord to grant you all the grace you need to get through this part of the Journey, but be advised, you will struggle.

Although we haven't spoken of Satan's activities for a while, do not get the idea that he is idly standing by. You can expect him to do anything he can to keep you from remaining faithful to your quiet time with the Lord. For me, getting very sleepy during prayer was a common occurrence. I could be wide-awake and alert until I approached prayer time. Then almost as if drugged, I would get sleepy and spend the entire time trying to stay awake. At other times, I struggled with distraction during prayer. A variety of things unrelated to prayer would come to mind. Things I hadn't thought about in years. My mind was difficult to control, constantly wondering off or thinking about things I could be getting done. Distractions are normal and you should not be too concerned with them since they are all a part of being human. When distractions come, simply pull your mind back to prayer.

Trying to be still before the Lord was really a challenge. By this time in my spiritual walk, I had developed a habit of going to the Blessed Sacrament nearly every day. For those who do not know, the Blessed Sacrament is a place in Catholic churches set aside for quiet prayer. For me, it had become very difficult to pray at home—almost impossible. It was much easier for me to pray when I removed myself from all the activities surrounding me and went to the Blessed Sacrament where I knew it would be quiet. Even in doing this, I still struggled with prayer. It was amazing how distracted my mind became whenever I would go to prayer. The constant effort to keep pulling my mind back to prayer would become exhausting. Not surprising, I did not feel very close to the Lord during this time. He was still silent and I did not feel his presence very often.

As mentioned before, in the fourth level of the "Wilderness" stage, we become acutely aware that we are not holy at all. We realize that we have a long way to go and that we must "die to ourselves." The phrase "die to self" means that we must allow the Lord to have a free hand to work in us interiorly so that we may be freed from all the things that prevent us from loving others and from being more Christ-like. It means trading hate for love, selfishness for giving, and pride for humility. It means displaying all of the fruits of the Spirit that will come as a result of the Lord's work in us. The self in us does not want to suffer or to be denied, and it certainly does not want to die. Therefore we can learn two things in this stage. The first is that the self has to die, and the second is that it does not want to. Hence, we continue to have a fierce interior struggle.

As we grow in the spirit, we will want to do what God asks of us, but the self will continually wants its own way. St. Paul gives us a glimpse of this condition. Turn to the Book of Romans, chapter 7 beginning with verses 14–19. Here is what St. Paul says in his own words about this level of the "Wilderness" stage: "We know that the Law is spiritual; but I am a mortal, sold as a slave to sin. I do not understand what I do; for I don't do what I would like to do, but instead I do what I hate. Since what I do is what I don't want to do, this shows that I agree that the Law is right. So I am not really the one who does this thing; rather it is the sin that lives in me. I know that good does not live in me—that is, in my human nature. For even though the desire to do good is in me, I am not able to do it. I don't do the good I want to do; instead, I do the evil that I do not want to do." He continues in verses 24–25: "What an unhappy man I am! Who will rescue me from this body that is taking me to death? Thanks be to God, who does this through our Lord Jesus Christ! This, then, is my condition: on my own I can serve God's law only with my mind, while my human nature serves the law of sin." In this reading, we can clearly see that St. Paul is struggling interiorly with the self in him and has come to the conclusion that his human nature is a real problem. For those who remain faithful, they too will come to this conclusion.

You can count on the Holy Spirit to be working hard in you during this "Wilderness" stage. However, if you get to the point where it seems as if you are just wandering around aimlessly and nothing is happening, know that something really is taking place deep inside of you. The feeling that nothing is happening is common, but eventually, the Holy Spirit will show you that He has indeed been working all along. Spiritual growth is sometimes so gradual that you don't know that it has taken place.

The way you will know that you have grown in an area is when you find yourself reacting differently to the situations in your life that previously caused you to get angry, resentful, bitter, or frustrated.

God does an enormous amount of interior healing in this stage as well. This too can occur without your even being aware of it until you find yourself thinking of a painful memory and discover that it no longer hurts. The memory may still be there but the pain is gone. So even though you do not see Him or feel Him, you should always remember that God is continually working in you. He is cleansing, purging, healing, and working to mold you into the saint that He has called you to be.

Time is another good example of this gradual growth. God gives us time freely, but a lot of people have difficulty giving it away to others. I was no different. When I was in the "Corrupting Forces of the World" stage, I spent all of my time doing what I liked to do. I didn't want to take the time to listen to someone who was having a lot of problems. A common statement in today's world is "You will know who your friends are when you run into a problem." The more serious the problem, the less you will see of them. When I reached the "Bondage/Egypt" stage, I became the person who needed someone to listen to me. The Lord sent someone from the "Wilderness" stage down to the "Bondage/Egypt" stage to help me. This woman had six children, but she spent untold hours listening to me, praying with me, and comforting me. I thank God everyday for this woman. Once I received my deliverance, I didn't need her time anymore. When I reached the "Wilderness" stage, something inside me changed because I desired to be the person that God could send into someone's life to listen to him/her. People in bondage require a lot of time. They are hurting and suffering. I wanted to be the person to go back there and tell them how wonderful it is over on the other side. On the Spirit's side of the field, life is no longer unbearable. I didn't care if it took a lot of time in prayer, listening, and comforting them. I knew I couldn't take away a person's bondage, but I also knew that I sure could be a light of the Lord's for that person surrounded in darkness.

After spending some time in the "Wilderness" stage it became clear that I had grown. However, exactly when it happened, I could not tell you. If the truth is to be known, back when I was in the "Bondage/Egypt" stage, I didn't care about other people's problems—I only cared about my own. I was not a loving person at all. You cannot love another unless you care first. No one will care what you say until you care enough to show it. Throughout my experiences in the different levels of the "Wilderness" stage, somewhere along the line, I became a caring person who loved to see God's goodness and mercy poured out on other people. I finally got to the point where I could rejoice in someone else's deliverance. I got to the point where I could put other people's needs before my own, and where I could be patient, loving and kind. Now that is spiritual growth.

Level VII: Running Towards the Goal

One of the more unusual symptoms of this stage is the issue of your health. I found this to be quite perplexing. What seems to happen here is that you will experience pain and symptoms of something being wrong with your body. It will tend to persist until you go to the doctor where all sorts of tests will be conducted. However, after evaluating the tests, it will be determined that nothing is wrong. This is unnerving because the symptoms are very real, and so is the pain. It will leave you wondering if there really is something seriously wrong. From experience, I can tell you that this is not unusual, and often times the symptoms will disappear on their own. I believe this to be another round of attacks by Satan. Satan never has or ever will stand by idly. A person in this stage is his enemy and since they are becoming more Christ-like everyday, they are a huge threat to him as well.

Control is another issue that is dealt with in this stage. It is human nature to want to control the affairs of your life. But to control your own affairs is not God's divine will. God wants to be the one in control. He cannot use you effectively as a vessel nor will you grow in certain areas of your spiritual life if you are constantly in control. The further you travel up the Spiritual field, the more aspects of your life you will be required to surrender to God.

When you were back in the "Bondage / Egypt" stage, the only thing that was surrendered to God was your big bondage and whatever was associated with it. However, there will be other things in your life that may not be affected during the "Bondage/Egypt" stage that will be affected during the "Wilderness" stage. Remember we spoke about taking all the interior bondages with us when we crossed over to the Spirit's side of the field? You can expect these to be dealt with here as well. For instance, many people harbor resentment in their hearts. Most are not happy with some aspect of their childhood. If you resented your parents, your social status, your economic situation, the lack of opportunities afforded you, an overbearing caretaker or an alcoholic parent, then now is the time that the Lord is going to root out the cause of the problem and purge the resentment from your heart. When you go through bondage, it is not unusual to harbor resentment towards the different people who have been instrumental in causing the bondage in your life. This too will be dealt with at this time in the Journey. We often struggle with the Lord here because it is not uncommon for us to try to justify the way we feel. If you have resentment, it means that there is still some unforgiveness in your heart, and you cannot advance to higher stages carrying this inside.

Bringing your mind under captivity to the Lord is another issue requiring attention. As long as your mind is not under captivity to the Lord, it behooves you to know that Satan can still use this avenue to stir up problems, cause you to sin, and get you to stray outside the will of God. Bringing your mind under captivity takes a conscious effort on your part. In the end, you want your mind to be totally under the Lord's control. If you continue to surrender your mind to God, eventually His thoughts will become your thoughts.

As mentioned, many things occur in the "Wilderness" stage. This text is only meant to give you some exposure on what to expect and some common experiences that people have in the "Wilderness" stage. It is in no way a complete explanation of everything that occurs.

It is important to mention some tips that might help you through this stage. First, the most common emotion that you will feel will be anger. You may even rebel against some of the lessons that you will have to learn. If you do, simply pick yourself up, dust yourself off, ask for forgiveness and continue on your walk. "There is no condemnation now for those who live in union with Christ Jesus" (Romans 8:1).

How are you to be sure that you are living in union with Christ Jesus? Obedience is the key. "But if we obey his word, we are the ones whose love for God has really been made perfect. This is how we can be sure that we are in union with God" (1John 2:5).

Secondly, if you are in the "Wilderness" stage (you will know whether or not you are by the symptoms you experience) you desperately need to have some type of fellowship with other Christians. A good Spiritual Director can prove to be a valuable source to you as well.

And finally, Satan, once again, is very active in this stage. The most common ways in which he works is through confusion and accusations. He will run before the throne of God and constantly accuse you of not living up to the standards set by God himself. The best thing you can do is to resist Satan when he makes you feel guilty or tries to get you to believe that God is angry or disappointed with you. God did not make us perfect, therefore, He already knows we have faults and shortcomings and He does not condemn us for them.

We are all leaving this planet someday. The choices we make here will determine where we will be for eternity. Use wisely your power to choose. It is a gift from God. Your ability to choose is a powerful tool that will bring the blessings of the Word of God into your life both here and in the hereafter.

To say the Wilderness experience is difficult is an understatement. You are learning to die to self and are struggling to become what God wants you to be. You are coming face to face with your true self. Back in the early stages of the Journey when you answered the call, the person you surrendered to the Lord was a person with problems both inside and out. The life you turned over to the Lord was filled with self-pity, anger, unforgiveness, resentment, bitterness and, of course, bondage.

As you can see, in the "Wilderness" stage, the Lord is working tirelessly to get you to the point where you are holy. Clearly He is showing you through your actions and reactions that you are not holy.

Don't give up, keep running towards the goal. God wants you to make it both into this stage and out of it. He will bestow upon you the grace you need to be successful. He wants to bring forth in you the fruits of the Sprit. In the early stages of the Journey, most people do not possess the fruits, however, by the time they near the end of the "Wilderness" stage, the fruits will definitely be evident in their lives.

The lessons you learned upon entering the "Wilderness" stage will be nothing like the lessons you learn as you near the end of the "Wilderness" stage and come closer to the "Promised Land" stage (see illustration).

LEVEL VIII: LEAVING THE WILDERNESS

As you near the end of the "Wilderness" stage you will know it. Struggling will be a constant part of your spiritual walk. Your spiritual side will want to please God and do that which is right, but you will keep falling and will continue to have to approach the throne of God seeking His forgiveness. You will realize that your response to God's love is woefully inadequate.

The self will continue to fight you because it will want things to go back to the way they used to be. The self will want to return to a time when it got what it wanted. It won't like being starved to death through self-denial. In this part of the Journey though, self-denial is crucial. The self must die. The only way to do that is to cut off everything that is feeding it. Then, and only then, will it begin to die. The struggle with the self comes to an end when it's dead, and for most of us that will take a lifetime.

The closer you get to the end of the "Wilderness" stage, the more you can also expect to experience what it feels like to be put to shame. Through no fault of your own, you will know what it feels like to be falsely accused (just like Jesus) or what it feels like to have your good character tarnished. Your acts of kindness towards others will go unappreciated. You will know what it feels like to experience unrequited love. You will know betrayal by those closest to you. The experience of feeling abandoned by those who are supposed to care about you is also common. In case you do not yet realize it, the Lord is allowing you to experience some of the same pain that He experienced in His passion. One thing is for sure, unless you have actually gone through this stage, you may not understand much of what you have read here. However, if you have experienced this level of the "Wilderness" stage, then you know what you have read is true.

Although this is a normal part of the Journey, it is indeed a very dark and painful period in your walk with God.

This is a word that the Lord gave me at this time in my own Journey. I think it bears mentioning here. On December 17, 1980, while in prayer, the words simply came and I wrote them down. I am revealing it here for the benefit of those who are currently going through this.

"Be ye present to the moment, even in your pain. Do not look for ways to escape the pain but rather look to the cross and in the cross find the strength and courage necessary until the work in you is complete. No student is greater than his master. One of the greatest lessons taught from the cross was how to be present in the moment of pain. Even if you do not understand, you must accept the will of my Father at all times. It makes no difference whether the pain is physical, mental, or emotional; all require that you be present to it every moment in order for it to be pleasing to the Father. Spiritual growth will bring all three types of pain together in the soul's Journey and lead that soul directly to the cross, where it will be nailed there as the soul continues to be submissive in surrendering everything to me."

These are powerful words which, as strange as it seems, gave me comfort because I knew that the Lord was allowing me to experience the same feelings He had in His suffering, and it was an indication that I was still on the right path. Through most of this experience, I resorted to reciting the entire passion—I memorized everything from Judas's betrayal of Jesus to the actual crucifixion. Then I would recite these scriptures almost everyday. These passages truly had special meaning to me as I was going through this part of the Journey.

What happens with the mind during this time is difficult to explain. The mind seems to be in a world all of its own. For me, there was a lot of forgetfulness, confusion, and an inability to concentrate. I could be reading the Bible, or a spiritual book, and after having read a few paragraphs, I would be unable to remember what I had read only moments earlier. In addition to this, trying to grow spiritually by attending conferences, teachings, seminars, etc. tended to be a futile effort because I didn't seem to be growing that way either. There had been a time in my life when I had grown enormously through these means, but at this particular point in my Journey, none of those things seemed to help me. It was as if the Lord was feeding me some other way. The evidence of spiritual growth was taking place, but I cannot explain how.

Up until this point, God had allowed me to grow spiritually, using my mind to feed my Spirit. Now it seemed as if He was no longer using this means. In other words, my mind was no longer the only method God was using to help me to grow spiritually. What is important to remember, is that you must put your faith and trust in the Lord, for you may not fully understand what is happening.

Throughout this process, I discovered that I had lost all confidence in myself, including my ability to explain anything to anyone. I really didn't welcome people asking me questions or looking to me for spiritual advice. However, what I did discover is that God gave me the words to help other people, and that I was not responsible for knowing what to say. In many cases, when you are approached by someone seeking advice, scripture will come back to your mind giving you insight on what to say.

Satan is actively trying to get you to give up and divorce God through this section of the Journey. He wants you to think that it's too hard and you can't make it. He desires to get you back on his side of the field where he is in control. But if you always remember that God knows what He is doing and will not give you more than you can handle, you will be successful.

It helps to not be ignorant of the tactics that Satan uses to get you to fall. He knows scripture and can quote it. He can give you anything you want and he will do it for a price. The cost will be your soul. In Matthew chapter 4, verse 8, Satan offered Jesus all the kingdoms of the world if only He would fall down and worship him.

Isaiah chapter 40, verses 27–31 will help you tremendously during this time. The passage reads: "Israel, why then do you complain that the Lord doesn't know your troubles or care if you suffer injustice? Don't you know? Haven't you heard? The Lord is the everlasting God; he created all the world. He never grows tired or weary. No one understands His thoughts. He strengthens those who are weak and tired. Even those who are young grow weak; young people can fall exhausted. But those who trust in the Lord for help will find their strength renewed. They will rise on wings like eagles; they will run and not get weary; they will walk and not grow weak."

The Lord has called you and He desires to work holiness into your life. It is His will for you to be holy. Every saint who has ever lived has walked this path to holiness. If you must, take each day moment by moment looking to God to help you through this stage of the Journey. He will grant you the grace and understanding that you need to succeed. If you get tired, don't worry because it's common to do so. Instead look to the Lord to strengthen you. Ask Him to stretch forth His mighty hand and fill you anew with living water that flows from His throne.

The Wilderness experience will change you. By this time in your spiritual walk, you will be determined to fulfill all the requirements set forth by the Lord. There will be a deep abiding love for the Lord in your heart. You will know that despite all outward appearances, the Lord's ways are truly better. And finally, people will obviously be able to clearly see the Lord in you.

The lessons learned by carrying the cross are invaluable for Christians. When you are ready to move on to the next stage, the way that you react, the way that you carry yourself, and the way that you are viewed by others around you will all be different.

Here are a few things that you will find different about yourself once you have gone through this stage. People can ignore you intentionally, and it will not hurt. Your suggestions can be completely ignored and it doesn't cause you to get angry. You will be able to take whatever the Lord sends your way, and understand that it is the will of God for your life and you will not try to escape it. You can be falsely accused, and like Jesus, refuse to defend yourself. You will be content with your life just the way it is. You will not be constantly bombarding the throne of God asking Him to remove some type of problem from your life, because you now know that it just might be a cross and you will therefore be able to accept it patiently, humbly, and without complaint. You will be able to confront evil and continue to stand firm. You will be able to see someone else prosper without any feelings of envy and resentment. You will be able to pray for others and see those prayers answered while prayers for yourself are not, and it won't make you feel slighted. You will no longer care what other people think about you. It won't matter whether others compliment you and speak well of you or not, because your sole purpose is to do the work of the Lord and fulfill His wishes for your life. You won't be unhappy with being taken for granted or overlooked. You will be completely satisfied with wherever God chooses to put you, and are able to minister to those around you, no matter how difficult the situations might be. You won't be dying to get noticed either. In fact, you might even feel more comfortable being in the background where you don't have to deal with the pride we sometimes feel when something we do comes off well. Finally, what seemed to be important to you has now changed. Therefore, many things that kept you filled with anxiety, worry, and frustrations cease to have a hold on you. You are now more at peace, because the Lord has freed you from all the concerns of this world.

The point when you actually leave the "Wilderness" stage and enter the "Promised Land" stage, it is not something you will be privy to. In other words, you will not know exactly when you move on to the next stage.

There is one more piece of advice I would like to share with you at this time. Since there are so many different lessons to be learned in the "Wilderness" stage, and since there are so many periods of profound confusion, it is very common to not know exactly what to do. Therefore you must surrender all your major decisions to the Lord and leave them there. This is not the time for you to decide that you are going to take matters into your own hands. It will be a major mistake on your part if you choose to do so.

CHAPTER VIII

THE CROSS IN OUR LIVES

Without a doubt, there will be a cross in your life in the latter stages of the Wilderness. This cross is a little different from other crosses you have carried in that it is a voluntary cross. This means that you will have a choice as to whether you wish to carry it or not. Many people do not recognize the situations that God allows in their lives as crosses, but rather see them as problems that must be solved. It now becomes very important for a person to be able to determine the difference between a cross and a problem. If it is a cross, we carry it. If it is a problem, we are to solve it.

There are eight signs that accompany a cross and which differentiate a cross from a problem. By carefully examining whatever situation is presenting itself in your life, you will be able to clearly tell the difference.

The eight signs that accompany a cross are:

1. It will be voluntary.
2. It will involve another person.
3. It will require a sacrifice for you to carry it.

4. Someone else will benefit from your carrying that cross.
5. Your carrying the cross will be foolishness to the world.
6. You will have a strong sense of unfairness.
7. You will feel used and abused.
8. The fruits of the Spirit will be developed in you.

There is no doubt about it, crosses can be difficult to carry, but you can depend on your Father in Heaven to be there right by your side through it all.

Everyday situations can help you to better understand the difference between a cross and a problem. So let us take a look at a problem. Let's say you are driving down the street and suddenly you hear a noise. Upon inspecting your car, you discover you have a flat tire. This is a problem, not a cross. When we apply the eight signs of the cross, none of them really fit. This is clearly a problem that must be solved.

Now let us take a look at some examples of crosses.

Suppose you have a child who is rebelling against everything in his life, is getting into trouble, is experiencing depression, and is clearly showing signs of anger. He is disrespectful, headstrong, doing drugs and drinking. You have a full-time job and a career. What do you do?

Taking a look at the signs of the cross, you can clearly see what the will of God is in this situation. If you were to quit your job and stay at home to spend more time with your child, it would be voluntary would it not? This fulfills the first sign. The situation involves another person and will require a sacrifice on your part, correct? Someone else (in this case, your child) will benefit from your carrying this cross. The very thought of your giving up your career will seem foolish to the world and you will feel like it is unfair that you have to give up your career for your child. The child has already demonstrated many problems and therefore it is highly likely that you will have experienced some type of abuse, be it verbal, mental, or emotional. Ultimately, the entire situation will produce the fruits of the Spirit in you. Some of these fruits are love, joy, peace, patience, kindness, and long suffering. Can you see how some of these very fruits will be required for you to carry this cross? These types of crosses always require that you put someone else's welfare before your own. The child did not get this way all by himself. There could have been a number of situations that occurred in his life in which he had no control that caused his rebellion.

In this situation, all the signs fit. It is a cross that God intends for you to carry. You'll never have to go out and look for the cross. It will present itself to you, and will challenge you to put the will of God before your own.

In many cases, it is not the person who brings the cross into our lives, but the circumstances surrounding them that does, and it is clearly not his/her fault. Consider this:

Suppose you are a career person who has an elderly parent. The time comes when it is no longer safe for him/her to reside alone. What should you do? If you apply the signs of the cross, it is clear what you should do. Sirach chapter 3, verse 12 of the New American Bible (St. Joseph edition) clearly states that children are supposed to take care of their parents when they are old. For some, this can get quite expensive, but when you were young, your parents provided for you, and it was expensive too. According to the thinking of the people in the world, giving up your career to care for an elderly parent is foolish. It is far easier to place him/her in a nursing home and go on with your life. However, according to chapter 3, verses 12–13 of the book of Sirach, unless there is some medical reason that cannot be handled by the child, the child is to " . . . take care of your father when he is old; grieve him not as long as he lives. Even if his mind fail, be considerate with him; revile him not in the fullness of your strength . . ." Nursing homes are never mentioned as a solution to caring for the elderly.

Yet another example of a type of cross to bear involves the blended family. In today's society blended families are commonplace. They can present all kinds of crosses for a Christian. So, let's consider a situation involving a blended family and apply the principles of the cross.

Suppose there is a couple that is not married but is living together. There is a child born into the relationship. The couple breaks up and the mother keeps the child. The father then moves away, meets, and marries someone else and has three children from that relationship. After a number of years, the first child's mother, unable to cope with life, turns to alcohol or drugs. The child now lives in a situation where he is being neglected and abused. The state takes custody of the child, places him in foster care, and then contacts the father to assume custody of the child. The father decides to do the right thing and takes the child to live with his family in another state.

The child is now eleven years old. He is angry about the whole situation and is rebelling against all authority. He does not recognize his stepmother as someone whom he must obey or respect. Life becomes miserable for everyone in the family. The father is quite passive about discipline and leaves all decisions up to the wife to handle. The child is constantly in trouble outside the home with neighbors and with teachers at school.

After a number of years, the husband, unable to cope with the constant arguments, decides to leave and does not take his eldest son with him. The child's natural mother cannot be found. The stepmother is a committed Christian. What does she do?

The first thing she needs to do is to determine if this is a cross or a problem. Then she will know what the will of God is for her in this situation. Is she to keep the child or allow him to be returned to foster care?

Again, applying the signs of the cross, she would first ask herself if it would be voluntary for her to keep the child. Of course it would be, since the child is not her natural child or her responsibility. The next question would be whether the situation involves another person. Yes it does! Will it require a sacrifice? Absolutely! Raising a troubled and rebellious child can be very painful and make you feel as if you are a sacrificial lamb. One can clearly see where the mother might feel used and abused. What about the fruits of the Spirit? Will caring for the child require love, patience, and long suffering? Yes! Would it seem foolish to the world? Certainly! Most people would think that she was crazy to take on a rebellious child rapidly approaching his teenage years who shows no love or respect for her. And finally, who is to benefit? It is quite plain to see that this is not a problem but a cross in her life.

Problems are never voluntary. We don't ask for them. They do not always involve other people. They do not require a sacrifice on the part of the Christian, and no one benefits from a problem. A flat tire is a problem, but in the above-mentioned scenario, the Christian was faced with a cross. God had allowed that child to be placed in her care. The child's future depended on the choices she made. The child had already been tossed around from foster home to foster home. He already believed that no one cared about him or loved him. This Christian woman could make a difference in this child's life if only she would elect to carry the cross. If she would bear in mind that God will not give her more than she can handle, and that He will be with her every step of the way, it would be easier for her to cope. And finally, consider this scripture: "Why should God reward you if you love only the people who love you? Even the tax collectors do that!" (Matthew 5:46).

As previously mentioned, scripture will always give you the answer to what you should do. Another scripture that is relevant to this situation can be found in Mark chapter 9, verse 37: "Whoever welcomes in my name one of these children, welcomes me; and whoever welcomes me, welcomes not only me but also the one who sent me."

There is another passage in the Bible that should be mentioned here. These scriptures had me confused for a long time until the Lord opened my eyes and allowed me to see. You will find them in Matthew, chapter 7, verses 21–23: "Not everyone who calls me 'Lord, Lord,' will enter the Kingdom of heaven, but only those who do what my Father in heaven wants them to do. When the Judgment Day comes, many will say to me, 'Lord, Lord! In your name we spoke God's message, by your name we drove out many demons, and performed many miracles!' Then I will say to them, 'I never even knew you. Get away from me, you wicked people!'"

I find these particular scriptures very frightening because Jesus is not talking to non-Christians, but to Christians. These people were casting out demons, speaking God's messages, and performing miracles. I asked the Lord, "What could these people have possibly done that you would say that you never even knew them?" The answer is that they rejected the crosses in their lives. We have no excuse for not carrying our crosses.

God's instruction to us has always been that if we want to be His disciples, we must carry our crosses. Crosses are never easy, nor are they fair.

Jesus voluntarily carried His cross. We reaped the benefits of His suffering. In your life, there are going to be many times when you will want to put that cross down, and you will feel justified in doing so. The self in you will continue to struggle against your carrying the cross. Satan will be constantly exposing you to reasons why you should not do it. You should ignore all of them. This is necessary in every person's Journey. All the saints who have walked the path before you have experienced this. God will grant you all the grace you need to be strong and persevering at this point.

It is interesting to note that for every cross

that exists, Satan has found a way to take that cross off your shoulders. He realizes the importance of a cross in a person's spiritual life. There are nursing homes for the elderly, day care for the children, juvenile detention facilities for the rebellious teens, and divorce for troubled marriages. Satan's ways have so permeated our society that it is considered completely acceptable to most people to treat the cross as a problem, and to solve it through the means that Satan has provided. Satan's solutions are never good ones. There is a lot of abuse and suffering in many of these places he has set up. The temptation will be there to take the easy way out; but if you do, Satan will have won.

CHAPTER IX

GRACE

Throughout the Journey, you must understand that grace is necessary to succeed in anything you do. It is essential to the Christian walk. So now it becomes important to understand exactly what grace is and how it functions in our spiritual lives.

Grace is God's favor bestowed upon us. This favor is completely undeserved, meaning that we do nothing to receive it. All grace comes from God. It is through grace that we have the ability to live the kind of lives we are called to live. It is also through grace that we receive all the help we need to be successful on our Journey towards God.

During the Journey, we are faced with hardships, crosses, insults, rejection, and painful situations that cause us to struggle. Trying to get through all this without God's grace is impossible.

Attempting to succeed without grace is the same thing as trying to watch television with no electricity. It simply will not work!

Everyone should ask the Lord for grace. The more difficult the situation you are faced with, the more grace you will need. Never hesitate to ask the Lord for this grace.

Mankind has strayed so far away from God through sin that it has become necessary for the Lord to bestow His grace upon us before we are capable of even wanting to turn away from sin and begin to walk the Journey. Therefore, grace had to have been operating in our lives long before most of us even realized it. It is through grace that our hearts are touched and the desire to walk the Journey originates. This type of grace occurs prior to any action on our part. It is the grace that is necessary for us to respond to God's call in our lives.

We previously spoke about the conversion process being continual throughout our spiritual lives—so too is God's grace. It is operating continually by moving in us and through us making us capable of living disciplined, Christian lives.

There are different means by which grace comes to us. Some of the most common ways are through the reading of scripture, the hearing of scripture proclaimed, through prayer, and through fellowship in a Christian community just to name a few. For Catholics, grace is also obtained through the sacraments.

One of the most enduring passages of scripture can be found in 2 Corinthians 12:7–10, which explains how grace actually works in our lives. In this passage, St. Paul is faced with a painful physical ailment. He prays three times for the Lord to remove it. God does not remove it, but rather grants him the grace to endure it. Read carefully what the Lord God says to St. Paul in verse 9: "My grace is all you need, for my power is greatest when you are weak." Then St. Paul says: "I am most happy, then, to be proud of my weaknesses, in order to feel the protection of Christ's power over me. I am content with weaknesses, insults, hardships, persecutions, and difficulties for Christ's sake. For when I am weak, then I am strong." What St. Paul is telling us is that the work of grace is what gave him the ability to endure all the things he had to experience throughout the time he spent in the Wilderness.

St. Paul received an abundance of supernatural help from God through grace that enlightened his mind and strengthened his will. This gift of grace will operate in your life exactly the same way. It will strengthen you and make you capable of choosing God's ways over that of the world.

Some of the more common ways in which grace touches your life is by helping you to do all the things necessary for spiritual growth. For example, it takes grace to go to God in prayer on a daily basis. Your human nature is opposed to this and so it is grace that gives you the ability to do it. Every time you go to a prayer meeting instead of watching television, it is grace that is operating in your life. Grace is responsible for your getting up and going to church on Sunday instead of sleeping in. All of these examples are, of course, a very simplified way of explaining how grace works in your life. Some of the more complicated ways are demonstrated when God is developing the fruits of the Spirit in you. For instance, for God to produce the fruit of long-suffering in your life is a very difficult task. Long-suffering means patiently enduring a difficulty or a struggle. It takes grace in order for you to be able to cope with whatever is going on in your life that will produce this fruit.

Grace is responsible for your continuing your walk, in spite of insults, shame, afflictions, tribulations, and generally all the things that our human nature dislikes.

It is the work of grace that enables you to turn your back on sin and all that it offers you. On the Spirit's side of the field, all the choices you make successfully usually require grace.

When surrounded by darkness, confusion, and a sense of being downtrodden, it is grace that gives you the ability to go on.

Much grace is poured out upon God's people when they are carrying crosses. You would be virtually incapable of carrying a cross without it. Your human nature seeks to take the easy way out when it comes to crosses, but it is grace that gives you the desire and strength to choose to be obedient no matter how difficult the situation may be.

Clearly, you will never die to self if you do not have grace. It is God's grace poured out on you that enables you to deny the self, turn the other cheek, and endure all the interior suffering that is going to occur as you walk this path with the Lord. The whole experience is painful, and it is only the grace of God that will give you the victory.

The Word of God says that our human nature is opposed to what God wants. In other words, what our human nature wants to do doesn't take grace—grace is needed for that which our human nature doesn't want to do.

Satan will actively try to stop you from succeeding on your Journey. You should know that it is God's grace that makes you capable of resisting Satan. Failure to resist him will result in his becoming more persistent in causing your downfall.

There is another type of grace called sanctifying grace. This type helps you to grow and to become stable in your new life. This one comes directly from the Holy Spirit. Its purpose is to make you holy and pleasing to God.

Obviously, grace is a gift from God that is absolutely necessary in a person's Journey. Do not be concerned about whether the grace will be there when you need it. God knows your needs before you even ask Him and He will provide for you as promised.

CHAPTER X

Words from the Master

Any good father notices when his child needs words of encouragement. Your Father in heaven is no different. He knows that sending you on this Journey will cause you to experience a wide range of emotions. He knows that you will not understand everything that you must experience. He knows that you are looking to Him to provide you with the guidance, knowledge, and instructions that you need.

In Joel chapter 2, verses 28–29, God is clearly showing that in the latter days He is going to be using His servants in special ways. The passage reads: " . . . I will pour out my Spirit on everyone: your sons and daughters will proclaim my message; your old people will have dreams, and your young people will see visions. At that time I will pour out my Spirit even on servants, both men and women."

In your quiet moments with the Lord, you will come to understand that He does speak to His people in a variety of ways. Sometimes He will use scripture, sometimes other Christians, sometimes dreams, sometimes the situations in your life will provide you with insight, and sometimes He will just speak to you directly.

If you have not reached this point in the Journey, then understanding how God speaks to you directly may be hard for you to grasp. For those who have reached this point, trying to explain it can be difficult. It is not an audible voice that you hear, but rather something that comes from within. It is important to remember that all you receive must be discerned before it is to be accepted. If it is from the Lord, then nothing in it will conflict with scripture.

When He speaks, it is always advisable to write down exactly what you hear exactly as you heard it.

I cannot speak for anyone else, I can only share with you my own experiences throughout this process of becoming a new creation in the Lord. I have included a number of messages I received from the Lord in hopes that it will help you. Each message provides you with the date it occurred. They are given exactly as I received them. I have made no effort to explain them, only to present them.

FOOD FOR THOUGHT
SEPTEMBER 1, 1989

"What would you do if whatever you attempted to do, for the rest of your life, you knew you could not fail?

Think about this. Would your attitude

change? Would you endeavor to do more? Would you move on to bigger and better things? Answer me—what would you do?

Understand this, my child; this is exactly the way I wish for you to think about the Spirit in you. The Spirit in you does not fail. Your heavenly Father does not fail. For those who are called according to my purpose, who are submissive to my will, who are attuned to divine wisdom, and who allow the Spirit to work through them, these can acquire this attitude: that in the carrying out of my will they will not fail.

Consider Moses. Did he fail? No. Think about my servants David, Joseph, and Paul? Did any of them fail? No.

You are called according to my purpose. Take heed and learn to walk confidently in my Spirit."

GOD REVEALS HIMSELF IN A DIFFERENT LIGHT
JANUARY 3, 1993

"You must come to know me and understand my ways. You must relinquish your very self to me, place your trust in me, and walk through the darkness with me before you can spend eternity with me. The seed I placed in your heart will grow. This seed comes but by my hand and creates in you that very desire to not only walk with me, but to also want to spend eternity with me. You are dependent upon me in all things. It is my desire to teach you all that is necessary for you to grow in union with me. Part of this teaching involves revealing myself to you. For how can I expect you to want to spend eternity with someone who you do not even know?"

INSTRUCTIONS
JANUARY 18, 1994

"Do not be disturbed when those around you insult you and keep you at bay. Learn humility. Use each situation towards your own spiritual good and your reward will be great in the hereafter. Offer the pain and hurt up to me knowing that I see all and know the motive behind each heart. Come stand with me before your accusers. Feel the pain as insults and accusations are hurled about you as I did. This is the lonely path that few take. This is the road you must take. Follow it. Know that when you reach this place, compassion, understanding and kindness are not things that are afforded you. For those who hurl the insults care not about your fate. Try not to explain your feelings to them or even defend yourself for their hearts are hardened and their eyes are blinded and they do not know what they are doing.

It is in this painful place that you will learn true forgiveness. It is in this place that you will attain freedom from grudges, jealousy, and inappropriate reactions to those around you.

I am here, very near to you now. I walk close beside you as you venture down this road of true darkness. Speak not evil of the actions of those around you even though their actions are from the evil one. Let not evil pass through your lips."

Lesson
January, 29, 1994

"Happy is the soul who refuses to listen to the self and pamper it. Turn a deaf ear to self for gratification and material rewards, for such behavior leads to greed and self-indulgence. Instead focus on the kingdom knowing that your rewards will be much greater in the life to come. All my faithful saints have learned this painful lesson and could effectively deny their very selves for my sake."

Surrender
February 1994

"If you do not relinquish a part of your life, I cannot take control of that part. Therefore it remains unhealed, in darkness, and full of pain. No one can become whole unless all of the parts of his self are surrendered.

It is you who determines how slow or fast this process will be by how quickly you are able to see what needs to be relinquished and by how quickly you take the necessary steps to do so. I can reveal your faults to you and open your eyes to see them, but it is you who must acknowledge them, confess them, and surrender them all to me. Do not blame me for the faults you see that linger for years. They are there because you have not surrendered them to me.

Worry, anger, frustration, fear, and resentment are faults you clearly see. They are all parts of who you have come to be. They are unrelinquished parts of you. You fear what you think I will do in order to get these out of you. Do you not see that fear is the biggest beast of them all. It overshadows everything you think and do and prevents you from surrendering all to me.

You long for wholeness? I tell you that this is what it is going to take—trust! Trust me to manage all of your life. Herein lies the true happiness you seek."

WORD GIVEN
AT A PARTICULARLY PAINFUL TIME IN MY WALK
FEBRUARY 1, 1994

"Do not run . . . Stand fast . . . hold on for your Savior is very near. You feel you cannot handle one more heartache, one more disappointment, or one more problem and you feel that my words to you don't really apply to your situation. But I tell you that they do. I will not give you more than you can handle, mentally, physically, or emotionally. I will not be untrue to my own words.

I have a mission for you in life and that mission requires endurance. Endurance is only acquired through the kind of trials I have allowed in your life.

Lessons in endurance tend to drive one to

the point of wanting to quit. Therefore I must proceed with caution. Know that my hand governs all, each trial, the intensity of that trial and the length of it.

You are at a crucial point—the point of wanting to quit. My demands of discipline, trust, fasting, dying to self, and surrender have, in your eyes, taken their toll. You feel you cannot go on, that you cannot bear even one more day. To deny that you can is to deny the existence of my power and grace to sustain you."

ANOTHER LESSON
FEBRUARY 2, 1994

"Now more than ever you need to place your trust in me. Have faith in the one who saves you. Like Peter when he stepped out of the boat, you see that there is no solid ground beneath your feet. The waters are rough and storm clouds seem to be all around. You see no way to get back to the safety of the shore. But I tell you that those whose faith has been raised to a higher level are as safe in the middle of the ocean as those who are on the shore. They know deep within their hearts that their shepherd will lead them to safety and green pastures. He will never abandon them.

Faith of this kind only comes to those who pick up their crosses daily, who learn that the trials and tribulations of life are but stepping stones to developing true divine character. It comes to those who humbly submit everything to me and believe that through me all things are possible. Those who accept these lessons with humility receive an out-pouring of grace that builds their faith to a heroic level.

These are the ones who can stand in the face of anything and still their faith is not shaken. Upon these, my favor rests."

REVELATION
FEBRUARY 2, 1994

"I have high expectations of you. It is you who have placed limits on what you can achieve. In me there are no bounds, in you there are many. Your entire future lies before me. I see clearly what you are destined to become. I also see every intricate detail of what must happen in order for this new creation to emerge.

As your eyes are being opened, you see the magnitude of work to be accomplished. You see the sin and your poor response to the work of my hand. But I've always known it was there and what your response would be. It is no surprise to me—only to you.

Begin to grasp this truth. How deeply I love you in spite of it all. Think of how valuable you are in my eyes. It is easy to fall in love with someone who is pure and beautiful. But I love you even with all your sin, faults, and shortcomings. Come to me just as you are and know that there is nothing there that will separate you from me nor that will cause me to stop loving you."

WORDS OF SOLACE AND COMFORT
FEBRUARY 10, 1994

"I am in love with my people. Therefore I take no pleasure in ever seeing them suffer; on the contrary, I suffer with them, hurt for them and cry with them.

I so love them that I laid down my life for their good. You find it difficult to forgive even the smallest infractions of those around you. But my love for mankind required that I look into the face of death and still cry out "Father, forgive them."

ENCOURAGEMENT
FEBRUARY 29, 1994

"Take courage, stand firm and fear not. Be ye unfearful of the challenges that lie ahead. For I have enabled you to stand in the face of danger and difficulties and not be harmed.

Courage is a quality desperately needed by many of my people who are crippled with fear. They are so bound that they are unable to carry out my will for their lives.

True courage means that you are able to walk in the valley of darkness and fear nothing for you know I AM. You'll not question that I am by your side.

Fear no man, fear no evil, and fear no difficulty. Know that my protection follows you wherever you go. How much safer can you be then in the arms of your Savior? I provide the shelter for you. Rest peacefully for I AM everything you need."

INSTRUCTIONS
MARCH 3, 1994

"Do not view this time in your life as wasted. To you, it is a time when nothing seems to be getting accomplished. In your eyes, nothing is better. You see it that way only because you are looking through human eyes. You must learn to see with spiritual eyes. Once you do, you will see that nothing is as it seems.

I know that you feel useless to me, as you are not actively working as you think you should. This is not the time.

When my divine plan unfolds before you, you will clearly see why it was necessary to set you apart in order to work in you and with you one on one.

Be ye patient and compare not your walk with that of another. It serves no fruitful purpose."

CALMING MY FEARS
MARCH 31, 1994

"I am watching over you, every moment of every day. My eyes are constantly on those who belong to me. I assure you that nothing you encounter along your Journey can cause you harm for I have placed your feet upon solid ground. It is only the doubt within you that causes the fear and panic you experience. It is you who take your eyes and place them on the circumstances around you. I do not remove from you the threat of harm—this I allow in order to build your faith and for you to grow in courage and strength. Do not fear the fiery arrows of the evil one. They cannot harm you unless you allow them to. Put on your armor and keep the faith and victory shall be yours."

COMFORTING WORDS
APRIL 22, 1994

"I am calling you to a higher place. Let go of all that is temporary and strive for what is everlasting. Everything is minute in comparison to the riches and glory in store for my people.

Fix not your eyes on the things of the world for they will pass. Don't look at the lives of people around you and wonder why I allow them to prosper while your needs go unnoticed. You must fix your eyes on the things above. In this way you will not feel that your choices were wrong and your life's struggles are in vain."

CORRECTION
JUNE 7, 1994

"The self in you is not dead. It is understandable that you are frustrated, angry, and full of despair as you spend day after day wrestling and struggling with it, and to you there seems to be no end.

Confusion abounds in your mind, for my

plunging you into total darkness does not seem to be an act of love to you, but rather an act of punishment. You seek for me to demonstrate my love for you on a human level by removing you from all pain, all suffering, and all disappointments, but I cannot. I am divine and my love for you will be demonstrated on a divine level, not a human one. Do not confuse the two.

For me to plunge you into total darkness is a profound act of love, for it means that I am very close and desire to become even closer to you, the one I love. Do not run from me. Stand still and let my love envelop you.

Your response to this is but the result of what your mind has been conditioned to think love is. For if another human brings pain, suffering, and disappointment into your life instead of happiness, contentment, and satisfaction, would you not be ready to run? I condemn you not for your response for I do understand that you see me exactly the same way.

The root of your confusion comes from what you see versus what I tell you. Can you not see that this is a lesson in faith?

For today I wish for you to remember this. The pain in our relationship is on both sides. I'm suffering too. The risk that is taking place now is on both sides too. You take the risk of losing all for me, and I take the risk of losing one so precious to me."

New Insight
July 21, 1994

"Any man who sets out on a journey knows not what he will encounter along the way. He can prepare himself well, plot out his course, and take every precaution to ensure his journey will be safe. But that does not mean he will not encounter danger or detours along the way. There is no guarantee that all will go smoothly and he knows it.

Why then, do my people who start out on their journey towards me expect everything to go smoothly and get angry when it does not?

Unlike the traveler, you have been told beforehand some of the encounters you will experience. Have I not told you that the road, which you must travel, will be difficult? Have I not already told you there will be trials and tribulations along the way? Have you not been warned of the enemy's potholes? Why then do you expect things to always go smoothly?

If a traveler is driving down the road and experiences a blowout, he is faced with a choice. One is to get out and fix it so he can continue on his journey and the other is to sit on the side of the road and complain about his misfortune. What is the better choice?

Unfortunately, the second option is what many of my people choose. They often- times spend years sitting on the side of the road complaining about the blowout and never even attempt to move on.

Complaining serves no good purpose nor does it solve any problems. So why waste the time doing it?

Allow me to open your eyes that you may see clearly what I wish for you to do and the choices I wish for you to make.

Never forget that I am with you always, my child, and there is nothing that you will encounter along the way that you and I cannot handle together."

INSTRUCTION AND UNDERSTANDING
AUGUST, 1, 1994

"Compare not what is happening in your life to that which is happening to others. In all of creation there is a law at work—a truth which makes all things come together in peace and harmony.

Picture in your mind a quiet, serene, peaceful, rolling hillside located far from the activity of man. The trees are tall and stately and the grass is plush and green. At first glance it may appear that nothing is moving and that nothing is growing, but nothing could be further from the truth. Much activity is taking place, activity that does not readily meet the eye. Activity governed by my hand, for the trees are growing so gradually that one does not even notice.

Likewise, growth is taking place in you so gradually that you do not see it and it appears that nothing is happening. In reality though, much activity is taking place deep within your very being.

Listen and listen carefully, little one. The trees on the hillside are untouched by man. Man did not prune them nor water them. The grass is plush and green. Man did not fertilize it, water it, or cut it, yet both the trees and the grass flourish and they are a beauty to behold.

I have placed you on the hillside far away from the activities of man. Here is where your transformation will take place, for you are completely in my care. Your growth will not be aided by or through man, but by my hand.

Compare not what is happening to you to what might be happening to a tree in the city where man's hand is permitted to aid in growth.

Long not to be a tree in the city where your views will be obstructed by the frailty of man. Instead, long to be a tree on the hillside, full of the power which flows from me.

Cease trying to be a tree planted in the city for you will continue to feel a misfit. Be ye content with your place on the hillside."

COMFORTING THOUGHTS
DECEMBER 23, 1998

"My dear little one, happy are you who place me so importantly in your life. It does not go unnoticed. Each soul such as yours holds a special place in my Sacred Heart.

My world is still beautiful to me. My

mountains of majesty, my beautiful flowers and trees, my mighty rivers—yes, they are all beautiful in my sight. It is only the sin of man that brings great pain and sadness to my heart. Blessed are they who see the condition of the world and pray for it. Mankind is in great need of my mercy upon them. Never before has this world been in such need as it is today. Pray, my child, pray. Know that your prayers are necessary to temper the anger of my Father. And as for you, enjoy the beauty of nature all around you. Don't take it for granted. It was placed there for your benefit.

Go in my peace and love, and remember I am counting on you to continue to be a light in so much darkness."

COMFORTING THOUGHT
DATE UNKNOWN

"I am in love with my people. My love is so much deeper and far greater than you can ever imagine. This makes me vulnerable to you. Anyone who is in love is vulnerable to the one they love. There are ways in which one can be hurt only if they are in love with another.

Remember this day always. For today I tell you that I am in love with you. When you tell someone that you love him or her, does it mean the same thing as being in love with them? Of course not! You may love a friend but it does not mean that you are in love with them. Being in love with someone suggests something far more intimate does it not?

Today, I call you to this Holy love; I call you into a relationship with me that is intimate. I want you to love me as I love you—a love so tender, so trusting and so fulfilling as to leave you lacking nothing. No one likes to be in a position of vulnerability, yet this is exactly what I have done for your sake. My suffering did not stop on Calvary. I suffer daily. Unrequited love brings much sorrow to my heart and the ingratitude by so many increases the pain.

This is why I do not wish for anyone to be lost. Does it not hurt to lose someone you are in love with? This is also why I go after my lost sheep. They are too precious to me to let go. My actions towards you will always be motivated by this intimate love. Oh how it hurts to know that there are some among you who feel alone and unloved. Believe this lie no more.

Today, my people I have revealed to you exactly how I feel about you. Now I ask you, how do you feel about me?"

CHAPTER XI

P̲RAYER̲

It must be emphasized that each stage of the Journey should be bathed in prayer. There are many different ways of praying, and you should expect your prayers to change as you advance through the different stages.

Obviously, prior to the "Bondage/Egypt" stage, there was very little, if any, praying going on in your life.

In the "Bondage/Egypt" stage, most of your prayers would have been petitions. This is normal. Most people in this stage do not know how to pray any other way. Also, the big bondage you were going through at the time caused you to cry out to God for relief from the pain. No prayer is going to be ignored by God if it comes from a sincere heart, no matter how self-centered the prayer might be. At this point, you were not worried about how you prayed, only that you did pray. The only thing that was necessary here was that your request did not violate scripture in any way. Over the years, I have been shocked to discover how many people actually pray for something that God simply will not grant them since it will require that He go against His own word. Here is a good example. One night in the early 1980s, following a prayer meeting in the Philippines (where we were stationed at the time), a lady came forward and requested special prayer. Clearly she was deeply troubled and in a lot of emotional pain. Her problem was that she had been having a protracted affair with a married man and they had just produced a child together. She was deeply in love with this man. Her prayer request was for God to intervene in the situation and cause the husband to leave his wife and three children and come to her. This violates scripture and she was actually asking God to condone adultery.

God will never answer that prayer the way she wanted Him too. In this case, I refused to pray for this to happen, but instead prayed that her eyes be opened that she might see the error of her ways and repent. I also prayed that the Lord would go before her and choose a husband for her and a father for her child. I've heard, so many times, a person say, "I've been praying for something for years and God just doesn't answer my prayers." Can you now see why this could happen? Have you ever heard of people expressing anger towards God for not answering a prayer and refusing to have anything else to do with Him because of it? Wouldn't it have been far better for them to examine their request against scripture than to walk away from God forever? God gave us scripture and put us in a place where we are free to read it. People simply cannot blame God if they are ignorant of scripture.

Once delivered, your prayer usually changes to thanksgiving and praise. For those who have been granted the gift of tongues, this is the way they usually pray. Notice that nothing so far shows any indication that you are listening to God. You are still doing all of the talking. However, by the time you reach the place where ministries begin, you will have usually started to listen. In fact you must listen in order to carry out the Lord's instructions regarding your ministry.

Once you reach the point where the interior work gets underway, your prayer will once again change. The way in which you pray usually depends on the stage you are in. Here, prayer becomes difficult and it will take a calculated effort on your part to succeed. Remember, the Lord is no longer feeding your feelings but developing your faith. It is not unusual for prayer to become more of a conversation with God.

One of the most profound ways in which the Lord speaks to me is through nature. Trees, ponds, flowers, gentle breezes, ducks, and birds have all played an important part in my spiritual walk and each hold special meaning to me. Let me share one such experience with you.

One day as I was working in my yard, I pulled up a tree that had previously been planted. It had died. I just threw it in the corner of the yard and continued to work. Then about a month later, as I was praying, I remember telling the Lord how dead I felt inside. Later that day, I went out into the back yard for something and happened to glance over at the discarded tree. I was shocked to see that it was showing signs of life. There were several buds on the end of the twigs. I was dumbfounded since the tree was not even in the ground and wasn't getting watered or nourished in any way. We live in Texas where the temperature can reach a hundred degrees or higher nearly every day in the summer. At that moment I clearly heard in my spirit. "Not everything that looks dead really is." This was a clear reference to the conversation I had had with the Lord earlier that day.

By the time you reach the deeper stages of the Wilderness, you will need to be aware of the many ways in which the Lord speaks to His people. The further you advance in the Journey, the more you become aware that it is not always necessary for you to speak. God already knows your heart. The more you know about the different ways that the Lord speaks, the more attuned to God you will be.

It is doubtful that any of us will ever experience talking to God like Moses did through the burning bush. That was a profound and unusual way in which the Lord chose to speak to His servant. For most of us, the ways in which God chooses to speak is not so grandiose. Take a look at Exodus 18, verses 13–27 which depicts a situation where Moses was exhausted trying to do everything alone. God used Jethro, Moses' father-in-law, to advise him on what to do about the situation. Moses took the advice and his problem was solved. This is similar to the ways in which we hear God speak today. God often uses other Christians to tell us something or to confirm something to us that He really wants us to know.

Scripture is also a common way the Lord communicates with His people. Good Christian books are another source that God might use in order to reveal spiritual truths to us. In short, He will use any method He can to get through to us.

During the Wilderness experience, you will discover that there is yet another way of praying. Up to this point, it is not unusual for you to not know anything about this method of praying. It is called Contemplative Prayer.

Contemplative Prayer is rooted in a person's desire for a deeper relationship with God and an unquenchable hunger for more of Him. It is the type of prayer that demonstrates that he/she wants a more committed prayer life and wants to be among people who are experiencing the same deep desire.

To contemplate means to look at or review with continued attention, to observe thoughtfully, or to consider thoroughly and deliberately. There are several different approaches that you can use in order to go into Contemplative Prayer. The first one is the use of scripture in which you take a particular passage and read it slowly and carefully. You then imagine yourself witnessing the events that are being described and actually visualize yourself in that situation. In doing this, you can evaluate your actions and your response to what is happening. This will also reveal to you your feelings towards the Lord. For instance, suppose you read the passage where Judas betrays Jesus. In your mind, you are there watching this whole event unfold in front of you. What are you thinking? Are you shocked and angry? Are you dumbfounded? Will you step forward? And what about Peter's bold action of drawing his sword and cutting off the servant of the high priest's right ear? What about the other apostles, what do you think they might have been contemplating in their minds? There are several scenarios that can be played out in just this one passage. This process can enlighten you about what is in your own heart and enable you to become aware of areas where changes may need to be made.

Contemplative Prayer involves having an awareness of the presence of God and focusing on Him. Little is actually said in this type of prayer. This is why it is also called a prayer of quiet. This type of prayer was a little difficult for me because my mind would be constantly distracted by thoughts unrelated to prayer. God, however, does have a way of getting through to me in spite of this. I recommend perseverance in this type of prayer because the rewards are great.

Going into complete silence before God and pulling yourself out of the chaos of the world around you is advisable no matter which way you choose to contemplate. Silence is not simply the absence of noise. You can remove yourself from ordinary sounds around you, such as phones, doorbells, television, radios, and the like, but not be interiorly quiet. Contemplative Prayer tends to bring a person to the interior quiet that is necessary.

The second approach you can use to experience Contemplative Prayer is the one that St. Teresa of Avila used. She simply sat attentively and quietly before the Lord and allowed Him to take over her prayer time. You should remember that the further you go on the Journey, the less you do and the more the Lord does in all areas of your life, including prayer.

The purpose of Contemplative Prayer is to guide you into the direction of interior quietness. Once you have reached that point, you can relax and allow the Lord to speak to you. Don't expect Him to speak to you every time, though. Often you will just rest and receive a renewal of your Spirit during this time.

Early in your walk with the Lord, you will have the tendency to spend your quiet time praying the way you want to. Surrendering your quiet time to the Lord is difficult because it doesn't feel like prayer. It is prayer, but not the kind you are accustomed to. For me, Contemplative Prayer was a struggle since my mind was so easily distracted. As mentioned, this is part of being human. What I've come to understand is that God is indeed nourishing us, but He is not using our minds to do it. I know this because I see spiritual growth in my own life which is not a result of the Lord's using my mind. Up until I made it into the "Wilderness" stage, my mind was a part of almost everything I learned. Now He seems to be teaching me in different ways that do not include my mind.

Our minds have a difficult time being still. They are accustomed to constant activity and don't exactly know what to do without it. I believe distractions are the result of our minds desperately trying to regain control of activity. If you do not understand this dilemma, don't worry; when you reach this point in the Journey, all of this will become quite clear to you.

Relinquishing your quiet time to the Lord's control is the key to not feeling as though you haven't accomplished anything. God's ways are different than ours. We must learn that if He is in control, then whatever He chooses to do or not do must be accepted in loving, peaceful surrender to Him.

I am an active person by nature, so sitting quietly before God requires a deliberate act of my will. I don't always succeed, but I do continue to try. On days when it is too difficult, I recite the entire passion (the portion of scripture covering

Judas's betrayal of Jesus up to the actual crucifixion) and stop and reflect on the different events that took place during that time. Over the years, I have recited this passage so often, I know it by heart. This may not work for you, but for me, it was certainly advantageous.

Still another approach to experience Contemplative Prayer is to surround yourself with religious articles in an effort to be able to focus on prayer and place yourself in a prayerful state. Surrounding yourself with these articles doesn't mean you are worshipping them. They are simply acting as an aid to place you in the right frame of mind. If gazing at the cross does it for you, there is nothing wrong with that.

For those who are serious about understanding Contemplative Prayer, another source of learning is through examining the lives of the saints and spiritual leaders in the Bible. Hebrews chapter 13, verse 7 states: "Remember your former leaders, who spoke God's message to you. Think back on how they lived and died, and imitate their faith."

If you will find books on the lives of the apostles, especially St. John (whom I believe to be one of the greatest examples of someone who was successful at contemplation who ever lived), and many other saints mentioned in the Bible, you will discover that they can teach you a lot about Contemplative Prayer.

For Catholics, many of the saints such as

St. Teresa of Avila, St. Theresa the Little Flower, St. Ann, the mother of Mary, St. Catherine, St. John of the Cross, and St. Augustine can teach you much about this type of praying. Study their lives and imitate the way in which they discovered how to come into the quietness of Contemplative Prayer.

For many, Contemplative Prayer can be difficult at first. No single method will work for everyone. It is best for you to try different approaches to discover which one works for you.

Prayer is a necessity in your walk with the Lord. It is the source of strength you will need. No student is greater than his master. If it was necessary for the Lord to pray, it is imperative for you to do the same.

CHAPTER XII

THE PROMISED LAND

St. Teresa of Avila, a widely-known and highly regarded doctor of the Catholic faith, tells us that in the higher stages of the journey we will not know exactly where we are as we continue to be obedient to the Lord. However, looking at the illustration, we know that we are coming close to our goal, which is Jesus.

The "Promised Land" appears to be a beautiful stage. I am not in this stage yet, so I cannot tell you what it is like. But in order to finish this book, I asked the Lord to reveal to me what He wished to say about this stage.

With the use of scripture and insight from the Lord, this stage seems to be one in which a person is completely content with everything in his/her life.

Thanks to St. Paul, we have a glimpse of what a person in this stage would be like. He describes such a person in Philippians chapter 4, verses 11–13: "I am not saying this because I feel neglected, for I have learned to be satisfied with what I have. I know what it is to be in need and what it is to have more than enough. I have learned this secret, so that anywhere, at any time,

I am content, whether I am full or hungry, whether I have too much or too little. I have the strength to face all conditions by the power that Christ gives me." St. Paul calls this condition a secret. It is a secret he learned by going through the "Wilderness" stage and by experiencing all the pain and suffering that comes with that stage. Clearly St. Paul is devoid of self. His self is no longer ruling his life. He has been freed from the worry of getting all his needs met. He reveals to us that he has the strength to face any condition using the power that God has given him.

Scripture never says that the Lord is going to fix the old self in us, but it says that He is going to make us a new creation. St. Paul became a new creation as this scripture describes. From the time he was knocked off his horse going to Damascus to persecute the Christians, until he reached this point in his life, is a good illustration of a person becoming a new creation. It is a process that didn't occur overnight, but instead one that took a span of many, many years to accomplish.

Obviously, when the Lord brings you to this point, you can be used as a vessel for anything. Mother Teresa of Calcutta is a perfect example of a person who had reached this stage. For those who do not know, Mother Teresa was a nun who had devoted her life to ministering to the poor in Calcutta. Though she is no longer with us, she was a prime example of a person who was not concerned about getting all of her needs met.

She had grown to the point that her own needs no longer mattered to her anymore. Her sole purpose was to serve the Lord through the people he placed in her life.

By the time you get to the "Promised Land" stage, the fruits of the Spirit will be clearly evident in your life. In Mother Teresa's life we can see love, kindness, goodness, joy, peace and patience. An account of her life and work can be found in many books in most libraries around the country.

Another characteristic of this stage is that you will come to the realization that you are totally dependent on the Lord. Although I have not yet arrived at this stage, I feel that way already. Perhaps I am simply experiencing a keener awareness of this dependence.

By the time you reach the "Promised Land" stage, it seems that you will also realize who you truly are. God himself has invested a lot of time, work, and energy in you. Throughout the Journey, there may have been times when it seemed as if nothing was happening at all, but by the time you reach this stage you will realize that in those times, God was indeed there and that He was simply working deep inside you. This is why it is imperative for you to continue to pray and be obedient to the Lord whether you feel anything happening or not. When you find yourself in situations where you react completely different then you did before, you can trust that God's work has been accomplished in you.

Another characteristic the Lord revealed to me about this stage is that people will come to the understanding that all their problems, perplexities, and questions are within themselves.

Like St. Paul, you will understand the authority God has given you and will know how to use it. It is easy to see that those who have come to this point are a big threat to Satan. By the time you arrive at this stage, you have spent many hours reading and studying scripture. You already know some of the authority God has given His people. But few people know how to effectively use it, which is exactly the way the enemy wants to keep it. However, God has other ideas. He wants His people to be able to deal with Satan just as Jesus did when He walked the earth. The Lord doesn't need an army of chickens; He needs strong warriors who are no longer fearful of the enemy. In this stage the tables have turned, for you will no longer fear the enemy, instead the enemy will fear you!

The presence of wisdom and understanding in your life seem to be still other indications that you have reached this stage. I am very grateful to St. Paul for having written the pages in scripture we so casually take for granted. They are a tremendous blessing to us because they allow us to see God's wisdom and understanding in the very things we must face as we travel the Journey.

People in the "Promised Land" stage can accept the fact that they are not perfect. St. Paul allows us to see that he came to a place where he understood that his human nature was wounded. He knew that God did not condemn him for that as long as he remained in union with Christ. In this stage, it seems that people are able to accept their limitations too. There is no jealousy, no unforgiveness, no resentment, and no bitterness in their hearts. They have learned to accept themselves just as they are and do not compare themselves with anyone else.

People in this stage not only know that the Lord loves them just as they are; they have also come to love themselves. You cannot love and accept others if you have not learned how to love and accept yourself. You learn this love from the Lord. It is an undying love He has for His people. You learn to accept and love others just as they are, too. We can see this in the life of Mother Teresa of Calcutta.

When you were in trouble valley, and God started to take the blinders off your eyes, and you came face to face with who you really are, you found that you didn't really know that person. And for most of you, what you did see, you did not really like. The average person is usually not satisfied with who he/she really is. There is always something that he/she does not like about himself/herself. However, in this stage you will grow to love yourself just the way you are. You must learn to love your neighbors as you love yourself. The order here is to love yourself first. If you are unable to accept the pot that the potter made, you will never be able to love it. Furthermore, you will never be able to love the other "pots" that God has created. This is one reason why you must go through all of these different stages. Your going through these different stages allows the Lord to work in you.

It is evident in Mother Teresa's life that she was capable of really loving others. She was able to minister to the sick and dying without a second thought. Most people want to satisfy not only their needs, but their wants as well. Mother Teresa could have decided to live the remainder of her life in quiet, peaceful abundance and turn a deaf ear to the cries of the people of Calcutta, but she chose instead to serve the Lord till the very end of her life. Living the life of abundance and comfort was not what was important to her. It had become more important to her to do the Lord's will and to love and care for the rejected, the downtrodden, and the poor.

There is a scripture in the Bible that reads: " . . . Do not be worried about the food and drink you need in order to stay alive, or about clothes for your body. After all, isn't life worth more than food? And isn't the body worth more than clothes?" (Matthew 6:25). I believe that until you reach this point, you will still care where your next meal is coming from. This is human nature. It is quite clear that we are simply not capable of doing some of the things that we read about in scripture until we reach certain points in our Journey, and even then we can only reach certain points after God does some major work in our lives.

By the time you get to the "Promised Land" stage, the divine has taken over and you are no longer concerned with anything expect pleasing the Lord. Through St. Paul we know we will come to the understanding that there is really no need to worry about anything, because we know that the Lord will take care of us.

In this stage, you can now live scripture to its fullest. You are truly free. You are also free from concerns about how and where you will live, and what kind of lifestyle you will have.

Obviously you can see that the transformation process has been ongoing for a long time. Otherwise, you would not possess these qualities. You should be able to see the difference between a person in this stage and a person in the "Corrupting Forces of the World" stage or the "Bondage/Egypt" stage. All the things that concern people in those stages are no longer important to a person in the "Promised Land" stage.

The next indication that you have reached the "Promised Land" stage seems very obvious to me as well. Your prayers have changed once again. You no longer offer up a long list of petitions. Since you are now basically content with your life, there is little that you will be asking for.

You will no longer be asking God to remove obstacles either. You will be asking God how to deal with them instead. You will be asking God for the grace to carry crosses, not remove them.

It is my heart's desire to make it to this stage of the Journey. It is also my prayer that perhaps the Lord will permit me to write about this experience when it happens. But until then, I cannot tell you anything else since I do not know.

CHAPTER XIII

THE JESUS STAGE

There is little I can say about this stage either, but I do know that upon arrival in the "Jesus" stage, you will be filled with the very nature of God. You will have the power to understand how broad and long, how high and deep, Christ's love is. You will come to know His love in a deeper way. This is described in Ephesians chapter 3, verses 14–21. By this point in the Journey, Christ will have made your heart His home. You will be truly strong in your inner self.

And so, my prayer for those who are reading this book is that God will bless you abundantly and give you the strength you need to successfully complete the Journey. It is also my prayer that this book has served to enlighten you and give you a sense that you are not alone when things happen to you throughout the Journey. I pray that God will grant you peace and determination each step of the way, as you walk surefootedly on unseen ground.

In scripture, David wrote one of the greatest verses ever written. He was a man whose faith in God had been strong and true. He wasn't perfect, and he had a lot of faults, but he was also a man after God's own heart. It is my prayer that everyone reading this book will feel exactly as David did when he wrote the 23rd Psalm.

THE 23RD PSALM

The Lord is my shepherd;
There is nothing I lack.
In green pastures you let me graze;
To safe waters you lead me;
You restore my strength.
You guide me along the right path
For the sake of your name.
Even when I walk through a dark valley,
I fear no harm for you are at my side;
Your rod and staff give me courage.
You set a table before me
As my enemies watch;
You anoint my head with oil;
My cup overflows.
Only goodness and love will pursue me
All the days of my life;
I will dwell in the house of the Lord
For years to come.

THE END

Contact Connie Porter
CONSTOP@stic.net
or order more copies of this book at

TATE PUBLISHING, LLC

127 East Trade Center Terrace
Mustang, Oklahoma 73064

(888) 361 - 9473

Tate Publishing, LLC

www.tatepublishing.com